From DearMonty.com

HOU$E
Money

AN INSIDER'S SECRETS TO SAVING THOUSANDS WHEN YOU BUY OR SELL A HOME

RICHARD MONTGOMERY

NATIONALLY SYNDICATED REAL ESTATE COLUMNIST

Dear Monty, LLC
PO Box 12434
Green Bay, WI 54307-2434
www.DearMonty.com

ISBN: 978-0-9984735-8-1 (Softcover)
        978-0-9984735-1-2 (eBook)

I want to dedicate the book to my family.

My wife and partner, Mary Jo, whose endless counsel, support and encouragement was important.

Our son, Mark, and our daughter, Erica, both of whom contributed their talents and energy to the project.

And to my co-workers, clients, customers, and readers who shared their real estate experiences with me to inspire this book.

ACKNOWLEDGMENT

WANT TO RECOGNIZE the 1106 Design team for their education and expertise in the design and production process and Write To Your Market.com for the book's title and sub-title.

CONTENTS

INTRODUCTION

THE SIX CHAPTERS OF THIS BOOK contain the foundation woven into the fabric of every real estate transaction. A real estate transaction is likely the most complex consumer transaction you will ever experience. The goal of this guide is to empower you to achieve better real estate outcomes. Possessing these insights will allow you to anticipate and prepare for each of the twelve steps in the real estate process. Just a few examples of better results are finding and managing an agent who produces results for you, knowing your way around contract language, getting accurate property pricing, and having zero costly surprises at the closing.

Because real estate transactions are a process—not an event—there are many more considerations in protecting your interests than these simple examples. At worst, a bad deal gone horribly wrong could cost thousands, or tens of thousands of dollars, and you may not even realize you were stiffed. Would you sell your house for $350,000 when it is worth between $375,000 and $400,000? Many real estate agents are not very good at evaluating homes. If you learn how to objectively evaluate a home, the chances of selling under the market decline drastically, as does the chance of overpaying for one. Wait until you see it is not difficult to do.

My unique background over decades in the real estate industry has provided me with rare insights into the real estate process. These insights have given me the opportunity to advise many buyers and sellers, as a practicing real estate agent, as the company customer service department (advising our agents' clients), and as an online voice of reason in the form of Dear Monty (www.DearMonty.com), a real estate Q&A column that appears in more than 500 newspapers throughout the country.

For decades, I have been answering consumers' questions about real estate—with more than two thousand Q&As online over the past four years, and I keep getting new ones! This book is my way of sharing even more information to a wider audience. I know your questions. I have your answers.

Experience has given me the insight and information I am passing on to you, as the real estate process unfolds. In this book, you will learn what actions to take—and to avoid—to achieve your desired outcomes. My goal is to never hear you say, later on, "If only I had known..."

Let me guide you through the six key points that allow you to better understand and manage each step through the process and why you need to learn these skills:

- How to appraise a home. Surprisingly, many real estate agents are not good at it.

- Understand the real estate environment. Don't be surprised by the rules and field conditions.

- How to hire a real estate agent. Consumers often do not have an effective plan.

- How to read a contract. Your agent may not explain it well—or even understand it well.

- How to collect and act on market information. Agents often disregard the importance of research.

- How to negotiate. Negotiation knowledge specific to real estate could be a game changer for you.

I began my career as a twenty-one-year-old real estate agent who only wanted to treat my customers as I would treat my mother and father. I had a strong, principled mentor who taught me his methods—honesty, knowledge, and efficiency. Yet early on in my career, I witnessed many disturbing situations in transactions that heightened my awareness that the consumer was at risk. Not everyone operated like my broker. I knew such abuses and errors were happening, but I did not know why.

Over time, experimentation with appraisals, inspections, and home mortgages offered new clues, but still the answers eluded me. I started a real estate brokerage model designed around the consumer rather than around the agent. I founded a corporate relocation company that outperformed the relocation industry by reducing our clients' costs using the same insights contained in these pages. I also consulted with Electronic Realty Associates (ERA), one of America's leading real estate franchisors, to introduce the ERA Sellers Security Plan™, which eliminates the risk of owning two homes when you buy a new one.

I wrote this guide because I believe that, when you implement the information described here, your efforts and new knowledge will translate to better outcomes for you by saving you money, reducing wasted time (which means money), and avoiding misunderstandings, lawsuits, and more.

Much of the real estate information available today is marginal, at best, and Internet articles can often be the worst sources of information (except those found on DearMonty.com, of course). For example, in an online article written by a real estate agent, the writer made the following statements:

- "The problem is real estate values do not change overnight." (This is false. Property values vary from buyer to buyer. Sometimes in the same day.)

- "Markets change gradually as market forces change." (False. Markets can change as quickly as new sales data become available, or as soon as corresponding news surfaces.)

- "Track records mean a ton in real estate." (Really? Some agents mislead customers to make their own track records look better or to make a sale.)

It is not just real estate agents who contribute to this problem. Major newspapers can unwittingly become victims to spreading inaccurate advice in their publications. The *Boston Globe* published an article titled "10 Things to Keep in Mind as You Weather the Home-Buying Storm." While there was helpful information in

the article, it also contained numerous insta⸱
misguided, or inaccurate information.

A blanket suggestion to potential home buyers to stay ⸱
from new homes, poor examples of questions to ask a seller, and
suggesting families overlook a nearby train track in favor of a
good school district may not have fit the circumstances of many
readers. Worse yet, *The Consumerist,* a division of *Consumer Reports,*
picked up the article, and it is still available for reader consump-
tion on their website.

In 2015, the National Association of Realtors (NAR) commis-
sioned an outside research firm to identify potential threats to the
real estate industry. That study, titled "The D.A.N.G.E.R. Report,"
asked real estate agents what they thought was the biggest threat
to agents. Their answer, "The real estate industry supports a large
number of part-time, untrained, unethical, and incompetent agents.
This knowledge gap threatens the credibility of the industry."
I believe it has damaged it already.

While agents like these are nothing new to real estate, what
is new is that the NAR appears to be thinking about the problem.
Having dealt with real estate agents around the United States
for many years, with both good and bad agents, is one of the
principal reasons DearMonty.com was founded. Dear Monty
does not have the means to research this next statement, but my
experience and simple calculations suggest that consumers of
real estate services lose more than a billion dollars *every twelve
months* buying and selling real estate. If these calculations are
even close, it is not something the NAR, real estate companies,
or victims will brag about.

The world of real estate is complicated. Much like the medical and insurance industries, service providers *do not have enough time* to discuss all the possible pitfalls with you. You need correct, trustworthy, and unbiased information *along the way* to succeed. With this book in your hands—coupled with the experiences and observations of Dear Monty—you now have a new ability to forge your desired path and achieve your real estate goals, and that makes me happy because, still, nothing brings me greater satisfaction than satisfied clients (and readers).

1

KNOW THE PLAYING FIELD

IN THE PAST FEW YEARS, more than ten million real estate transactions took place each year. Half of those transactions involved home buyers, and, of course, the other half were sellers. You are going to be one of those ten-plus million people buying or selling or both.

In terms of dollars, the residential real estate industry is one of the largest in the United States. Let's say the median price of a home is $224,000. With so many properties changing hands, this volume adds up to more than a trillion dollars in real estate value each year.

Real Estate Companies

The agent population constantly changes depending on the source of the information. There are about two million licensed real estate agents in the United States, according to the Association of Real Estate License Law Officials (ARELLO). More than a million licensed agents are members of the National Association of Realtors (NAR). The 2015 economic census reports 86,004 real estate companies in

America. The bulk of the million licensees who are not members of NAR likely are not practicing real estate at all. If a licensee is practicing and is not a member of NAR, exercise caution, and learn why the licensee is not a member.

According to NAR, 80 percent of real estate firms have one office and two agents, while the remaining 20 percent are larger. The largest firms have hundreds of offices and thousands of agents.

The vast majority of brokerage firms engage agents to work as independent contractors. Independent contractors are not "employees" of a company, even though it might appear so to a consumer. They are not held to certain working hours or work procedures the way they might be as an employee. Real estate companies like the independent-contractor relationship because the Internal Revenue Service treats independent contractors differently from employees. As a result, brokerage firms have limited direct influence over the agent-client relationship or the quality of customer service, which is one reason you need to be proactive when you decide on an agent.

Some brokerage firms have affiliated with national franchise brands, such as Keller Williams, Electronic Realty Associates (ERA), Coldwell Banker, Prudential, and RE/MAX. The franchise brands often are parts of even larger companies that license their brand names and trademarks and provide other marketing support to member brokerage firms.

NRT (formerly National Realty Trust), which is a part of Realogy, is the largest real estate company in the United States, with 47,000 agents in fifty of the country's hundred major cities. Other companies, such as Berkshire Hathaway, both own and franchise large real estate companies and rebrand them under the corporate name.

As in many industries, there is an inherent risk in real estate that human error will cause harmful errors or misunderstandings. This risk is a result of a number of fundamental industry characteristics:

- Consumers are not able to gain direct access to Multiple Listing Service (MLS) information. Local MLS is the only accurate source for real-time information.

- Consumers often alter their requirements. For example, buyers look at $300,000 homes until they learn $250,000 is their limit.

- Agents and consumers may misinterpret, falsify, or miscommunicate data. When we take shortcuts, rush our speech and writing, or don't listen and clarify, events can go terribly wrong.

- Agents may not be well trained, properly managed, or well suited for the work, and consumers are often ill prepared, with rudimentary industry knowledge. It can be like the blind leading the blind.

- There are multiple sources of data, but with no rules standardization. For example, many people do not realize they do not become first in line by submitting an offer on a home. Knowing this now may change your negotiating strategy.

Could these points contribute to the real estate industry consistently being one of the top sources of consumer complaints as compared to other regulated industries in the United States?

This is true in Wisconsin. The Wisconsin Department of Safety &
Professional Services has verified this fact, which is similar to an
inquiry made more than twenty years ago.

Each state that collects consumer-complaint information
has different methods of collecting and disseminating this type
of information, but Dear Monty suspects Wisconsin's real estate
complaint experience is the norm. Further, many consumers do
not report abuses either because they do not want to take the time
involved, are embarrassed, or believe nothing will come of it.

When Property Changes Hands

According to the NAR, back in the 1880s and 1890s, real estate
agents would meet together at "Real Estate Exchanges" to share
information about their listings. One can only imagine, but it
sounds much like the way the Chicago Board of Trade operates
today—open bidding in a free-for-all atmosphere. This was how
property was bought and sold. I would not be shocked to learn
they used three-sentence, handwritten contracts. Sometime very
early in the twentieth century, the term *multiple listing* was introduced, and by the time the 1920s rolled around, the term *multiple
listing* was widely accepted.

In 1975, the industry adopted a computerized Multiple Listing
Service, known as the MLS, to improve the system further. One of
the primary benefits offered by an agent to consumers is access to
MLS home listing data. Because consumers do not otherwise have
direct access to these data, the agent has primary control over the
process of searching and filtering MLS data.

Today, locally updated MLS data are available within minutes,
depending on the local MLS rules. According to NAR, there are

more than 700 independent MLS systems in the United States, operating on many different MLS platforms.

There is no substitute for a well-trained real estate agent who is pulling data directly from the source. When the Internet became a greater part of the real estate industry, the MLS found a new source of revenue: selling its listing information to other services. These services, or aggregators, which are also known as syndicators—such as Zillow, Trulia, Realtor.com, and many others—are scraping data from hundreds of multiple listing services, each utilizing one of many MLS software vendors. While the NAR is working toward standardization, the current lack of it among the MLS systems and vendors creates frequent information gaps and errors.

Not only do the large syndicators scrape data from MLS systems, but local real estate companies also have access to sharing MLS information on their websites. In the last decade, the Internet has become the first entry point for 90 percent of home buyers into the real estate market. No wonder: You can shop while sitting in your living room. Many of the companies posting MLS listings online also have developed mobile applications to make searching for a home even more convenient.

Another variable in the industry is a multitude of service offerings brokers utilize to promote and attract customers and clients to their firms. From the traditional full-service brokerage firms to transaction brokers offering only MLS access, and everything in between, the hype and sales pitches can be confusing for the consumer of brokerage services.

Finally, real estate companies use multiple methods to compensate agents. Some, but not all, real estate businesses and agents promote their compensation theories as part of their sales pitch with anecdotal productivity and service claims that can further complicate a home buyer or seller's agent selection decision.

Agency Overview

Every state has laws about agency and agency relationships. These laws vary in theory and specificity by state. You must seek specific advice from agents you are interviewing about how agency relationships work in your state.

The driving force behind the disclosures and changes in agency law over the past twenty-five years is fairness. In the days of *caveat emptor*, the buyer was at a disadvantage. The burden of discovery was on the buyer, and it still is in some states. *Caveat emptor* is Latin and means "let the buyer beware." In many states, if a buyer confides in the listing agent when they make an offer that they will pay more for the home, the listing agent has a duty to share that information with the seller. Other states utilize dual agency, which allows an agent to represent both buyer and seller. When dual agency is utilized it would not permit the listing agent to share it.

From a home seller's point of view, they are represented in an agency relationship immediately in the listing contract with the broker. The broker is the agent of the seller. The listing agent cannot tell a buyer that the seller shared that they will take less unless the seller grants permission.

The difference today is that real estate agents and brokers must explain the differences in agency relationships to all buyers and sellers. These disclosures must take place before any negotiation begins, and the states may not agree on what triggers negotiation.

Dear Monty recommends questioning multiple agents in the interview process, to follow in chapter 2, because personal experience suggests there is confusion about agency in the real estate industry, in part because it is hard to explain agency in all of the particular circumstances in which it can impact a real estate transaction. Even attorneys and courts do not always agree on interpretations of the law.

Buyers in the marketplace today may engage a buyer broker before they start looking, or when they find a home they want to make an offer on, or they may choose not to engage buyer broker representation at all. If a buyer looking at a home listed for sale by a broker has not signed a buyer agency agreement and the listing agent they met at an open house is the person they are working with, they must make a choice between representation or to remain a customer. If they remain a customer, in some states, the seller must agree to allow his agent to facilitate the transaction. If they want to continue working with the listing agent as a client, the seller must also agree. Again, each state is unique, so determine early how agency works in your state by seeking multiple opinions.

The listing agreement in many states requires the seller to make an agency decision when the home is listed. The decision a seller makes at that early point may be required to be amended later when a buyer discovers the home and wants to submit an offer. The decisions the buyer and seller make on agency may have implications in the transaction.

You will find questions and answers throughout this book, chosen specifically to illustrate often difficult-to-explain concepts, like this one on agency agreements. These Q&As come directly from real buyers and sellers who have posed these very questions to Dear Monty. Names and obvious identifiers have been changed to preserve privacy.

ASK MONTY

Tim Asks: I signed a contract with a buyer agent. We found a house and made an offer. The house failed the inspection, but the seller had the right to cure (in other words, fix the problem). I was not comfortable and walked away. Now my agent wants to enforce the buyer agency agreement. I talked to my attorney, and she questioned the strength of the agent's demand and said the purchase agreement was not well drafted. The list was $184,900; the offer, $199,000. What do you think?

Dear Monty's Answer: Not being an attorney, I cannot give an opinion on a legal matter. Consider taking the buyer agency agreement and the purchase agreement to a second attorney. If both lawyers concur, your agent is in a weak position, and you will have to decide which direction to take. It may be helpful for you or your attorney to try to negotiate a reasonable settlement, or you may choose to tell the agent "No" and see what happens.

The Contract Controls

The buyer agency agreement in my state is five pages long with 235 lines. Contract wording from state to state can vary, but the controlling sentence, picked out of a paragraph from our WB-36 buyer agency contract, dictates what happens in Wisconsin. "Broker's compensation remains due and payable if an enforceable written contract entered into by Buyer per lines 26–29 fails to close."

Many states have similar contract language. In your state, this clause may be the source of the contention. Wisconsin WB-1, the exclusive right-to-sell form, commonly called the listing contract, has similar language. Controversy over success-only fees on the WB-1 listing contract also creates similar situations.

A Typical Occurrence

It is likely that the majority of real estate brokers and agents fail to point out the meaning of this sentence to their client. While this is the sentence that is impacting you now, there are hundreds of circumstances that could occur in the real estate process. It would take hours to identify and explain each "what-if" scenario. It is also likely that consumers do not read the contract or do not understand the implications. Realistically, most transactions close without this fee issue. But when this issue presents itself, it is an unwelcome surprise.

So What Is a Buyer or Seller to Do?

The best solution for consumers is to read every document before you sign. This transaction is likely the most important in your financial affairs. You now know an enforceable contract triggers payment to the broker, so in the future, remember to ask the broker/agent if that sentence can be modified to read that the fee is due only when there is a closing. Many brokers would be open to that change when they are negotiating for the listing or a buyer agency agreement. They would likely balk at amending the agency contract after the problem appears because they have done the work.

When a buyer or seller refuses to honor the contract, the wording discussed here in the agency agreement will often be the transaction's saving grace. When faced with paying a pre-agreed fee with nothing to show for it, many reluctant participants will go to closing.

Agency law that concerns duties to each party, timing of disclosures, and agency choices can be difficult to apply. The law is complex. Circumstances that arise in a transaction can be complicated, and many real estate agents, including buyers' agents, cannot adequately explain agency law. Add crucial deadlines requiring very quick responses, oral discussions, and representations, and it's a recipe for confusion and misunderstanding.

The Devil in the Details

Multiple representation is not a factor in agency relationships unless both the buyer and the seller are clients of the same real estate company. If a buyer does not have an agency agreement with a real estate company, the buyer, then known as a customer, simply relies on the duties all brokers and agents have to all parties in real estate transactions. Again, the laws in each state as to the obligations of a broker to their client may contain subtle differences. Seek opinions from multiple agents. You may be surprised at the answers.

Generally, these are the duties of the agent without a buyer agency agreement:

- To be fair and honest in the treatment of buyer and seller. Questions must be answered honestly.

- To provide reasonable skill and care regarding market conditions, real estate law, and third-party recommendations, such as title companies, home inspectors, contractors, to name just a few.

- To disclose "material adverse facts," which are facts a consumer cannot detect on his or her own that materially impacts value or may cause the buyer to pay a lower price, such as knowledge the adjoining property owner is applying for rezoning next week. The only exception is when the agent is prevented from disclosing by law.

- To keep facts in confidence when asked, unless the agent is prevented from confidence by law.

- To provide accurate market condition information, which includes accurate statistical market data and does not include a value opinion.

- To safeguard all funds and account for them during a transaction.

- To objectively present all offers, with an unbiased presentation of pros and cons.

The Seller's Agent

An ethical, knowledgeable, and efficient real estate agent can deal with both sides of a transaction in an equitable fashion. How do you know if an agent possesses these characteristics? The best way to enhance your chances of fair treatment is to choose your agent wisely. "Wisely" means interviewing three prequalified agents.

- Prequalified means you have observed the agent interacting with clients at open houses. Or someone you know and whose opinion you respect and who has transacted business with the agent is recommending the agent to you. Or "informed witnesses" recommend an agent. (Dear Monty says "informed witnesses" are people who work in an environment where they see agents at work. These witnesses may be attorneys, home inspectors, mortgage lenders, and closing officers at companies that handle real estate closings.)

- Interviewing means asking questions designed to bring forth clues of honesty, knowledge, and efficiency from the answers and testing the candidates in the process of making your selection.

Examples of testing the agents could be

- Requesting advice about tasks you can undertake to position your home to sell. Should I have the home pre-inspected? Do I have to thin out my furniture and belongings?

- Asking prospective agents to research the market and share their opinion of the best price you can expect and the lowest price you should expect. Many of the important questions to ask can be found in the next chapter, with more on the DearMonty.com website.

The Buyer's Agent

A buyer's agent, or buyer agency, relationship is established when an agent searches for properties for a specific buyer utilizing an agency agreement. The buyer signs a contract for representation in buyer agency, much like a seller signs a listing contract for representation when selling. Buyer agency has gained somewhat in popularity and has circumstances in which it can be particularly useful, such as when you are purchasing a home in a new city.

For instance, if you share with your agent that you are willing to pay X more for the home when you make your initial offer, and you have not signed a buyer agency agreement, in some states, the agent will pass that information along to the seller. In theory, if you have a buyer agency agreement, the seller will never know you are willing to pay more.

However, buyer agency on its own is not a guarantee of smooth sailing. The best way to proceed with this choice is to include an exclusive buyer agent in the initial interview process. There is a difference between an exclusive buyer agent and a buyer agent. An exclusive buyer agent does not accept listings and does not work with a buyer as a dual agent. Most buyer agents are switch-hitters. They also work with buyers as subagents, dual agents, or transactional agents. The less you want to know about real estate as a buyer, the more appealing buyer representation may be to you. Hiring a buyer agent does not nullify or change the need to interview multiple agents. Do not wait until you are ready to negotiate for a particular home to interview agents.

Also, be aware that many buyer agency agreements provide that the buyer has responsibilities that are absent if they choose to remain a customer. For example, the language in Wisconsin WB–36 states, "Broker's compensation remains due and payable if an enforceable written contract entered into by Buyer per lines 26–29 fails to close." WB–36 also states, "Broker's compensation from Buyer will be reduced by any amounts received from owner or owner's agent." The implication of the first sentence is that you will incur obligations to pay brokerage fees if the transaction does not close. In the second sentence, it states the buyer must come up with the fee difference if there is a shortfall in the commission collected by the buyer agent from the owner or the owner's agent from the amount stated in the agency agreement.

Be certain you read and understand the buyer broker agreement because a buyer cannot depend on agents spending the time discussing the implications of these two sentences with you. There are 235 lines in Wisconsin's WB–36 Buyer Agency/Tenant Representation Agreement.

If you have a buyer agency agreement, get direction from your agent before you walk into an open house without him or her that will protect you and your agent at the open house from a "procuring cause" dispute if you decided to buy the house. If the open house agent wins the procuring cause dispute and is therefore not required to pay the buyer agent, the agency agreement you signed states that you will pay any shortfall.

Procuring cause is a real estate term that dictates the agent that introduced the house to the buyer is entitled to the commission. Anecdotally, there are stories of buyer agents who "sign up" buyers and do little work to find a home; the buyer disengages but does not get a release from the contract. When the buyer ultimately buys a home, the buyer agent reappears, looking for the commission.

From the consumer's point of view, it is helpful to be able to find information quickly, and with little effort, so the transparency the Internet offers is a good thing. On the other hand, be aware that online real estate listing sites generate their revenue through various types of advertising, one of which is revenue generated from real estate agents. Real estate agents pay for top billing on these sites, just like they do when they advertise in a newspaper or magazine. It is not always evident whether the agent listed next to a listing is the listing agent or is even familiar with that neighborhood.

Research from the NAR indicates that, in recent years, more than 90 percent of consumers choose an agent rather than trying to buy or sell without an agent. Whether buying or selling, the bulk of all consumers recognize that avoiding an agent to save money can be even riskier, more time-consuming, and may not save money.

For example, a couple looking for a home searches online for homes "for sale by owner (FSBOs)" and makes appointments to look when they find homes that sound interesting, one or two at a time, until they find one they want to buy. They hire a lawyer to draft a contract and make an offer 10 or 15 percent under the asking price because they've heard that is how to start a negotiation. Why would they do this? Because they believe they will save money eliminating the agent. They have chosen to forgo looking at a large percentage of all the homes on the market that are listed with real estate companies.

Now think about the seller's position in this scenario. They place a "for sale" sign in the front yard, advertise in FSBO magazines and online FSBO websites, and exclude the majority of home buyers who are looking in the MLS. Saving the commission is the seller's goal as well. Unfortunately, they both can't save it. Both the buyer and seller are limiting their selection, which is contrary to the law of supply and demand. The irony here is that even if they ultimately negotiate and close a contract, it is unlikely either of them will know that they actually saved money.

The Rules of the Game

Most of us coming into the real estate market today are searching for information. We tend to look for information about homes, neighborhoods, and financing. Consumers do not always ask the right questions because they do not know which questions to ask. Conversely, agents do not realize what we know and do not know. They are focused on determining what we want.

Dear Monty's intention is to provide you with information on many important, rarely discussed subjects including the "Rules of the Real Estate Game." Who sets the rules? What are rules meant to accomplish? Understanding these rules in advance should help you work more effectively within the system.

Who Sets the Rules?

The rules regarding real estate industry practices essentially come from four sources.

Department of Regulation and Licensing (by State)

Real estate brokers and agents are granted a license by each state. It is the responsibility of this department to monitor brokers and insure that they maintain acceptable standards of conduct. This department and its citizen board (often comprised of brokers) not only grant licenses, they also administer tests, act on complaints, and discipline licensees who are guilty of not following the rules. This is the principal source of regulation and is intended to protect consumers from incompetent, dishonest, and illegal activity on the part of the industry.

The Federal Government

The federal government has the responsibility of enacting, educating, and enforcing fair housing laws throughout the United States. The fed is also involved in legislation regarding financing of real estate where government agencies such as the Federal Housing Administration (FHA) and quasi-government financing agencies like Fannie Mae and Freddie Mac buy mortgage loans from lenders on the secondary market. These laws are intended to promote equality and fair treatment of all consumers, including "protected classes" of consumers when buying and selling real estate. These laws are a part of why a real estate agent cannot disclose information on protected classes.

National Association of Realtors (NAR)

Usually, but not always, licensed brokers and agents are members of the NAR. The job of the NAR is to seek, recruit, and educate members and to lobby for legislation favorable to the interests of their members and to a lesser degree the interests of homeowners. They promote the value of their organization to consumers, drive leads to their members at Realtor.com, and maintain a code of ethics for all members to follow. The rules they establish impact the procedure agents may utilize when dealing with the consumer.

Local and Regional MLS

While the MLS originally was organized by NAR, NAR distanced itself from MLS to maintain individual MLS independence and practice independent oversight and operations. A local MLS is separate from the local boards of Realtors. The local organizations establish and maintain rules that govern brokers in cooperative selling arrangements between members. Those MLS rules between brokers impact the consumer in the procedures that have to be followed when buying and selling a home or other property.

General Rules

Here are some general rules that are beneficial to know beforehand. These are general rules that brokers and agents must follow. These rules have been established by the aforementioned organizations to promote order and protocols, while promoting an orderly purchase or sale.

- Agents are not allowed to solicit listings while they are listed with another agency.

- Under a doctrine called "procuring cause," the agent that was instrumental in introducing a property to a buyer is entitled to the sales commission.

- All documents must be signed by all parties involved with the transaction.

- Fixtures stay with the property unless the parties agree that the seller may take them. Personal property does not stay with the property. For information on the difference between fixtures and personal property, refer to the fine print definitions in the listing contract or purchase agreement in your state.

‣ In addition to the sale price, the buyer and seller both incur additional customary closing costs, unless those costs become a point of negotiation or incentive one party offers another.

‣ Any agent that is a member of the MLS can show and sell any home listed by any other MLS member.

‣ In many cases, your agent will not know if there is another offer on a property.

‣ Although a property is listed for an established price, there is no law or rule preventing a buyer from offering to pay more or less than the listed price.

‣ When a home is listed, the listing agent is the only person who can consult with the seller unless the listing agent grants permission or the seller initiates a conversation with a third agent about his circumstances.

Rules Regarding Offers

Because making and receiving an offer is the most critical point in the transaction, most of the remaining rules relate to offers.

‣ The offered price and terms should be known only by the buyer, the agent who wrote the offer, the agent who presents it, and the seller.

‣ Sellers should be notified of the existence of an offer as soon as the buyer signs the offer.

- Offers should be presented in a timely fashion and in person.

- Buyers should be kept informed as to the status of the offer.

- Although circumstances vary and sellers usually want a long time to deliberate and buyers want the seller to decide quickly, twenty-four to forty-eight hours is reasonable in most cases.

- All terms must be described in writing on the agreement.

- Preprinted, state-approved forms are the only legal way an agent can draft an offer.

- No offer is legally binding until a copy of the accepted offer is presented or mailed to the buyer.

- Either party may withdraw or modify an offer prior to acceptance and delivery by or to the other party.

- There is no legal priority as to which offer is considered or dealt with first. The seller can even choose to sell to a buyer who offers less.

- The broker is obligated to present "any and all offers" to the seller by law unless the seller instructs otherwise.

- Counter offers are in effect rejections and do not give a buyer priority regarding negotiations.

Additional Insight

The information just discussed is an overview of the key rules that brokers and agents must abide by and should help prevent misunderstandings. My experience is that these rules do not become a part of the conversation unless a misunderstanding over one of these rules arises during the process. You will probably learn about additional rules as you proceed with your transaction. Each region throughout the country may have variations of these rules. Ask your agent in the location where you plan on transacting business if there are any additional rules and if these rules apply. The best time to ask is when you are interviewing agents.

Dear Monty believes only a small percentage of consumers have all the skill sets, available time, knowledge, and best contacts required to navigate the complicated real estate process alone. Additionally, most buyers and sellers would be further ahead spending the time they invested in viewing FSBO homes or showing their own home FSBO by learning about how real estate works, how to evaluate it, and how to execute each step in the real estate process. While there is much inefficiency with the current system and the MLS system, it is Dear Monty's opinion that the MLS is the best system yet devised to identify the home of your dreams or find a qualified buyer.

In summary, the industry is highly fragmented, internally focused, improperly trained, experiences high turnover and burnout rates, suffers with low entry-level requirements, and is lacking adequate supervision. The barriers to competition are low, which allows new entrants with minimal training and experience to break in.

For these reasons, the key to protecting your hard-earned dollars is to arm yourself with the knowledge required to make the right choices along the way. One of the most important choices is to learn how to pick the best agents with whom to work. There are very good real estate agents across the entire country, but it requires diligence and effort on your part to identify them. Chapter 2 will show you how to look beyond the fancy watch and luxury car sported by some agents to appear successful.

2

CHOOSING YOUR ADVISORS

FINDING THE RIGHT REAL ESTATE agent can make all the difference in the quality of your home-buying or home-selling experience. The agent you choose must be able to wear many hats, and the real estate process takes time. Bear these facts in mind, as you will spend much time with the person you choose.

You will want to consider many factors when analyzing the best time to enter the real estate market. If you have influence over timing your real estate move, the following suggestions can help you make the most of it. Timing can impact you both positively and negatively. Place each of your considerations into one of two categories: market conditions and personal circumstances. An objective evaluation of your personal circumstances and market conditions will allow you to make a more confident decision regarding the timing of your purchase or sale.

Under the Circumstances

No matter what the market conditions are like, usually buyers and sellers first consider their personal circumstances before making their decision. Your circumstances, such as your financial ability, emotional status, and time constraints, most often dictate when to buy or sell. Here are some specific events that may influence your timing:

- Retirement

- Marriage or divorce

- Employment promotion or transfers

- Serious injury, illness, or death in the family

- Conflicts with neighbors or landlord

- Desire to improve your surroundings, your needs, or your standing in the community

- Need for a tax shelter

- Children move out

- A new baby or a graduation

These and many other individual life events have an impact on your decision to buy or sell. Whether negative or positive, each of your personal details should be considered.

It is smart to be measuring your motivation. Measuring means to consider your entire situation to determine more accurately how practical it is to buy or sell. You should evaluate your financial ability, your individual needs, and your personal desire.

It is the overall interpretation of a combination of your present circumstances that will help you draw the right conclusions. This equation assists in depicting this concept:

$$\text{ABILITY} + \text{NEED} + \text{DESIRE} = \text{MOTIVATION}$$

Who Knows What the Market Is Like?

The real estate market is the other factor to examine. Knowing the market will often affect when you make the move. A retiring couple, for example, may have time to consider market conditions thoroughly before deciding when to sell their home. A homeowner who is transferring to another city for a job probably will not have that luxury.

When analyzing the best time to enter the real estate market, consider these general thoughts on the key market conditions to be aware of. In addition to real estate agents, talk to other vendors you will have to make a choice on as you go further in the process. Home inspectors, title companies, home builders, and mortgage lenders will all be happy to offer you opinions, as you are seeking to understand their role in real estate transactions.

Real estate agents can be reliable sources when they provide complete, unfiltered MLS data that you both decipher together. Be mindful in your instruction to the agent that you value unfiltered data. Only after understanding the unfiltered data can you determine which filters to utilize. Filtering data is very useful, but it is also a point in time prone to miscommunication.

What Information Should I Be Looking For?

It is particularly helpful to obtain an understanding of the current market conditions in your area in order for you to decide the

importance of market conditions. The key market considerations
are these:

- Fluctuations in interest rates: Waiting for interest rates
  to rise or fall should not be your only consideration.
  Declining interest rates can create a "seller's market," and
  your interest rate savings may be offset by an increased
  price. Conversely, rising rates can give way to a "buyer's
  market" as the number of qualified buyers decreases.
  Waiting for interest rate fluctuations may not be a chance
  you want to take.

- Average market time: Sellers should be aware of the average length of time it currently takes to sell a home. Buyers
  may want to compare present averages with prior norms.
  The average market length can be an indication of a seller's
  or buyer's market.

- Current and future economic trends: Consider the area's
  employment outlook, property taxes, and other community factors such as school district effectiveness. A leading
  company layoff or constant property tax increases in a
  community can negatively affect the market in that area.

- The law of supply and demand: By considering the number
  of competing properties versus an estimate of the number
  of people looking, the sales rate is a good indicator. You
  can get an idea of the current balance between supply
  and demand. Remember that different price ranges and
  different neighborhoods can be very different from the

summary of the total market. This information is available through most, if not all, MLS systems. Some agents understand the value of these data; others do not. Knowledge of the sales rate is one of the skills you want to be able to take advantage of when selecting your agent. Here is a sample of helpful information that can save you time and improve your decision-making arsenal. MLS software has the ability to produce multiple reports utilizing the data produced every day with the many activities generated by local market forces. Ask for information like this during your interviews.

	Average Active List Price	Median Active List Price	Average DOM active listings/sold listings
High value large city			
Single Family Under $1M	$629,307	$589,867	109/84
Single Family Over $1M	$1,874,203	$1,256,346	147/103
Condo/Townhouse Under $500K	$327,239	$304,875	87/76
Condo/Townhouse Over $500K	$890,756	$683,935	74/68
Average value large city			
Single Family Under $500K	$329,307	$289,876	109/84
Single Family Over $500K	$774,203	$656,346	127/103
Condo/Townhouse Under $250K	$227,239	$204,875	87/76
Condo/Townhouse Over $250K	$290,756	$283,935	74/68
Average city			
Single Family Under $300K	$289,307	$259,876	109/84
Single Family Over $300K	$474,203	$456,346	147/103
Condo/Townhouse Under $250K	$227,239	$204,875	87/76
Condo/Townhouse Over $250K	$265,756	$263,935	74/68

Figure 1. Overall market performance

Is Timing Important to You?

There are many aspects to consider before deciding if the time is right to buy or sell. After you have reviewed this information, you may want to make up a personalized list of pros and cons. Discuss market conditions with your contacts; check online, and talk to real estate agents to search for relevant data. The more information you gather, the better prepared you will be to move in the proper direction.

It's wise to interview at least three qualified agents before you choose one. This may seem like extra time and work, but the vetting will pay off. Your agent becomes your real estate counselor, your best information resource and your messenger, and you want the right one for these reasons:

- Buying real estate will likely be your largest single financial transaction.

- Some real estate agents are highly skilled; others are just overconfident or overcommitted. Others are lazy, dishonest, or not the sharpest knives in the drawer. Following the tips, exercises, and insights throughout this guide will show you the difference.

- All real estate transactions consist of twelve separate steps that often require different skills. In most businesses, employees are trained to deliver specific skills in a specific order. You wouldn't expect to go to a hospital and have a surgeon greet you at the door and admit you, because it's not an efficient use of resources. But in real estate, the agent must be involved in all twelve steps. If, or when, the agent falls short in delivering the service a particular step requires, you, the consumer, are likely to experience a gap in the quality of the service. As a former real estate broker who was the go-to customer service representative at the company, I can testify that a gap in service anywhere throughout the process can, and does, cause frustration, confusion, and financial distress.

- As independent contractors in an industry with low barriers to entry, agents often are left with little direct supervision. The financial structure of the industry cannot support adequate staff to oversee the agents. The broker in many real estate companies is the top producer, which restricts the time the broker needs to train, manage, and supervise agents. Further, often the broker has little direct formal management training to guide the agents from an organizational point of view. The larger companies expand by adding agents and buying up competitors, so the ratio of management to agent could be as high as twenty to thirty agents to one manager/broker. Many management gurus in other industries believe that a manager's limit on the "span of control" for supervising a sales force is seven individuals.

- Real estate training is misguided. The majority of the training is about finding and converting prospects into customers. There are training companies that teach agents how to "look" successful in how they dress and specific words in scripts to utilize when engaged with a potential customer. Instead, the training should be focused on appraisal techniques, customer service, negotiating skills, and construction techniques, among other important aspects of delivering a quality experience.

If you have a relative, a coworker, a friend, or an acquaintance from your place of worship who is a real estate agent, you may be tempted to pick that person to be your agent simply because he or she is familiar. Consumers may not understand the importance of picking a good agent, and it is easy to pick someone you know. According to the NAR, fully two-thirds of home sellers talk with only one agent. Dear Monty's experience suggests this is a mistake. But it is understandable, especially since it's tough to know in advance how any agent will perform.

If you have actual working knowledge of how this agent conducts business, you have more to go on, but engaging this agent because he or she is a "nice person" and you have some sort of connection has little to do with competency.

Dear Monty recommends going ahead with supplemental interviews as well. If your familiar choice stands up to the other agents you interview, you'll be far more confident in your selection.

Interviewing agents is the best way to predict future behavior. Asking the right questions (and the best follow-up questions) will help both parties better envision the relationship. Many people do not realize the interview is a double interview. Many agents are interviewing you as well. As you are evaluating them, they are deciding whether or not they want to work with you. Many agents have pre-set circumstances they are looking for, such as certain neighborhoods, price ranges, types of property, desire to only work with sellers, or buyers and more. Your interests will be better served if you take the responsibility to determine, as best you can, what to expect before engaging anyone.

What to Look for in the Interview

Consider each of your prospective agents carefully. Fortunately, there are questions to ask and qualities to look for when formulating your opinion. Focus on how each agent listens, how willing he or she is to answer your questions, and the quality of their responses. You cannot overlook personality, but quality advice and quality time are of utmost importance. If the agent is not on time for the initial meeting, cuts you off before the interview is over due to another appointment, or gives you trite or shallow answers, this behavior is not a good indication of things to come.

Keep your interview notes to refer to if a conflict should arise with your candidate of choice later in the process. The notes will also be useful if your agent interviews are spread over a period of time.

Where to Conduct the Interviews

If you are selling, invite the agents you have prequalified to meet at your home. This setting gives you a chance to observe their reactions to the property without any obligation. Using your home also provides you the opportunity to ask them to tour the house, make suggestions, and offer their opinion on the home's range of value. The "range of value" is the highest amount you *could* expect, down to the lowest amount you *should* expect. Use those exact words when putting the value question to each agent: "What is the range of value I could expect and should expect in the sale of my home? I want a range."

If you are buying, your current abode is typically the best spot to meet. It is your environment and is a quiet, secure place to have a conversation with minimal interruption. If you have children or pets, arrange for help so you can focus on the task at hand. Agents you interview can also develop a sense about you—your needs and wants and other factors that may help them maximize their efforts for you.

There are times that it's simpler to use a coffee shop or the agent's office for an interview. When this is the case, the quality of the dialogue between you and the agent is even more important, since the environment itself won't provide any helpful hints.

To illustrate this point, a couple once came to my office with a map that contained a highlighted boundary and strict instructions not to bring any information about homes outside that boundary to them because she did not drive. Their children's school was in the center of the map and within walking distance of the boundaries. Twenty showings within the stated boundaries and many months later, I was invited into their apartment for coffee after another failed showing. I noticed a framed photograph of them posing in front of a field of young spruce trees and inquired about the photo.

She said, "My parents own a Christmas tree farm." Later at my office, I found a Christmas tree farm for sale in a small community about fifteen miles from the school and told them about it. The rest is history. After the closing, I asked them about the long drive to school. The response was, "She's going to get a driver's license." They considered property outside their stated requirements because a new connection (the tree farm) was introduced to the search through a family photograph in their home.

These questions for agents can help you discern the differences among your prospective agents (and their companies). The questions are meant to be a starting point and to inspire more questions. Your conversation, your queries, and the answers received should be helpful to you in making a sound choice. When asking three agents the same questions, you will be surprised by the differences in the responses you receive.

12 QUESTIONS TO ASK PROSPECTIVE REAL ESTATE AGENTS (AND THE SMART ANSWERS YOU SHOULD EXPECT)

1. **What qualities set you apart from other agents, which benefit your customers?** You want to hear about the expectation they have of themselves for their clients and their perception of how the industry works.

2. **What kinds of real estate training and continuing education have you received?** Their general level of education and training geared toward helping the consumer, such as an appraisal course, would be helpful. Is the company behind them?

3. **Why is company support you receive beneficial to your customers?** Do they understand the value of company support and how it helps you as a client? If they see no support or cannot articulate it, this does not create a good feeling.

4. **What is your position on home inspections and home warranties?** Inspections are valuable in all transactions, and a home warranty depends on the home's age, condition, the coverage, and the home warranty company itself.

5. **What backup support is available when you are out of the office or on vacation?** How are your interests protected if you cannot reach the agent? The agent's reaction to your question, "I'm here 24–7," is not the answer you are seeking. You want to have the name of the

stand-in who will make time to honor your requests in your agent's absence.

6. **Can you provide the name and telephone number of three references?** Not a good sign if you cannot talk with their former customers. When an agent tells you that to supply contact information is illegal with the new privacy laws, ask if their statement is true when the agent has asked their former customer/client for permission. This small example is an indication the agent may not be well informed, may be a bit lazy, or may be intellectually challenged. It also may mean he or she does not have many satisfied customers.

7. **What is your company's track record for average market time and rate of listings not sold during the listing's initial term?** It is helpful to know the answer because "market time" does not consider unsold listings, and reduces the value of the data. This question creates work for them. Will they respond, and with a nonfiltered, MLS-generated answer?

8. **What services, if any, does your company offer that is not provided by your competitors?** Can they articulate some reason their company stands out? "Each week, we meet for a forty-five-minute mini-learning session on drafting contracts led by our broker" is a real answer. No real answer, such as, "They have me, and I am the number-one agent in the city," is a red flag.

9. **How do you establish your opinion of value for a home?** Knowledge check. Do they adjust for differences between features of the comparables? Do they find the same style of home, such as a ranch, if the subject property is a ranch? Or do they use some online algorithm-based appraisal? If the agent does not know how to pick good comparable sales and make adjustments between those comparables and the subject property, his or her opinion is suspect.

10. **How do you find your customers?** Sources, like open houses, they name that require effort on their part are a positive indicator. Referrals from other customers are good. A poor answer is, "People just come."

11. **Does your company have a satisfaction guarantee?** You are looking to see how hassle-free it will be to remove yourself if the relationship sours. "Our broker will release you from your listing contract" is a very good answer. If they cannot state some example of differentiation, start wondering about their ability to make sales.

12. **How quickly can you email us recent "sold" comparables?** How well does the organization communicate with you? The best answer is, "We can put you on autopilot." As a buyer, this means when a new listing that meets your requirements comes into the market, a link to a data sheet hits your inbox. If you are a seller, when similar homes you are competing with sell or go pending, you are notified through a link to the MLS.

For example, question 9 is one of the key Dear Monty questions: "How do you establish your opinion of value for a home?" The point of asking this question is to probe for an agent's knowledge and experience in valuation techniques. If one agent's answer is, "I go to Zillow and do a Zestimate," while another agent's answer is more along the lines of, "I find the best MLS-sold comparables in the neighborhood and make cost adjustments for the differences between each comparable and the subject property," it will be clear to you the agent adjusting values on comparable sales has a better grip on how to evaluate a home.

If you are a seller, and all three agents utilize comparables and adjustments, you will be able to judge their evaluation skill level when you review their opinions of the best price and lowest price to expect for your home. As a buyer, ask for a redacted example of one of their evaluations for a client.

Based on comments I have heard from agents in the field and comments I have received from readers, there are real estate agents who will answer that question with the Zestimate. When there are many similar homes within blocks of the subject property, a Zestimate may be fairly accurate some percentage of the time. When there are few nearby comparables, the range of value can widen appreciably. I am of the opinion that Zestimates, or any method of placing a value on a property where a real person with specific training in the appraisal methodology has not physically inspected the property, is not reliable.

Some agents may like Zestimates because it shifts any value responsibility away from them and also saves them the effort of doing the actual work. It may be good for them, but it is not good for you.

ASK MONTY

Rebecca Asks: Monty, we are preparing to sell our home, have gone through your recommended steps to find an agent, and are now down to two candidates. They both present as knowledgeable, hard-working, and efficient. What differentiates them in our eyes is one is very tech savvy and the other is more traditional in their approach. Is a tech-savvy agent a big advantage for us?

Monty's Answer: Technology and innovation have affected the vast majority of people in the United States. The impact of technology on the different segments and industries varies, and real estate is no exception. While real estate agents who have embraced today's bells and whistles would likely answer "Yes," the answer is "it depends."

Not many years ago newspaper ads were one of the primary lead generators for agents to hook up with home buyers. Today most hook-ups start online with real estate websites because of the convenience of both mobile and home access. Both print and online media are expensive for the agent to utilize in finding the buyer, but does the seller care which medium generated the customer?

What Is Different Today?
The speed and capacity of data transmission are the primary change agents that have allowed the cell phone and the Internet to drive innovation. While it is very clear that mobile devices, email, texting, software applications, and

other products have helped improve efficiency, it is less clear that technology helps sell individual homes. Here are some factors to consider:

- One of the most common pitches a home seller will hear describes featuring the home on many websites in addition to the local MLS. Video tours online are another relatively recent example. Some agents offer individual-property websites, devoted solely to your home. The cost of production can be very pricey with these promotions, but will a buyer pay more for the house?

- Real estate agents may choose to embrace technology and be early adopters or be on the other end of the spectrum and still not own a smartphone. Technology is only one of many facets involved in being successful in real estate. John Naisbitt's 1999 book, *High Tech/High Touch*, reminds us that there is no substitute for human interaction and personal relations. Many customers have not succumbed to technology, so if you prefer to speak with your real estate agent as opposed to texting him or her, it would be an appropriate follow-up question to ask both agents. What good is having an agent with a smartphone if the agent does not return calls promptly?

- What real estate agent is not interested in generating more revenue? A lot of agent training and software applications are about how to identify, convert, and maintain customers. These tools focus on convincing customers to work with them. Two examples are workflow automation software to eliminate time-consuming tasks, and customer relationship management (CRM) programs that rate and manage leads with the help of email, direct mail, and call centers. The direct consumer benefit of these products is not easily defined. All the effort to master and maintain these products can go out the window if the agent shows up late for appointments.

- The tale of the tape. Consider seeking the production numbers of each of the agents. Watch for conditions that can skew raw numbers. An agent with repeat customers can throw a lot of productivity on the board with less effort. For example, if one builder accounted for 50 percent of one agent's transactions, this is not a fair comparison. The team approach can also affect production, but it does not necessarily translate to increasing your chances of a sale. If four agents are sharing the workload and pooling results, it is not an equal comparison.

Seek the MLS production record printouts of each agent in the past twelve months that demonstrate how many listings are still active, how many expired unsold, and how many sold and closed. Real data may help answer your question in determining the effectiveness of technology in helping sell your home. If an agent is using his or her production as a benefit to you but is reluctant to share their record, it is a red flag. Many agents like to be asked about their production. Here is an "agent production record" below in Figure 2.

Firm / agent sales report
Report parameters

<date of report>

Date range:　　　　　<search from ___ to ___>

Sort by Agent Name: <yes or no>　　Board: <Name of MLS region>Firm: MLS #5972 <name of real estate company>
Report for Original List Agent: <yes or no>　　　　　　　　Agent: <name> (MLS 893285)
Report Totals Only: <yes or no>　　　　Office: 0

Credit Multipliers: <1 Listed>
<1 Sold>
<2 Listed and Sold>　　　　　Listing　　　　　　　　　　Selling

MLS #	Address	Firm	Agent	Price	Firm	Agent	Date
R90645482C	718 Vanguard	5972	893285	$263,200	2850	109751	02/04/2016
R27193642C	5986 Valley	5972	893285	$263,200	4590	399750	02/04/2016
R30135988C	2246 Larry Dr	5972	893285	$263,200	2965	909759	02/04/2016
R30135041C	3167 Brown Ln	5972	893285	$263,200	0765	689753	02/04/2016
R30136760C	1103 Kim Ave	5972	893285	$263,200	2850	179752	02/04/2016
R90136906C	3088 Ridge	5972	893285	$263,200	2877	489751	02/04/2016
Total	6 Units	Listed		$1,579,200			
R50122948C	318 Vande La	2850	109751	$263,200	5972	893285	02/04/2016
R50132842C	5986 Valley	4590	399750	$263,200	5972	893285	02/04/2016
R50135988C	2246 Larry Dr	2965	909759	$263,200	5972	893285	02/04/2016
R50135041C	3167 Brown Ln	0765	689753	$263,200	5972	893285	02/04/2016
R50136970C	903 Kim Ave	2850	179752	$263,200	5972	893285	02/04/2016
R50136713C	4088 Ridge	2877	489751	$263,200	5972	893285	02/04/2016
R50136713C	9088 Ridge	2850	109751	$263,200	5972	893285	02/04/2016
R50136713C	3088 Ridge	4590	399750	$263,200	5972	893285	02/04/2016
Total	8 Units		Sold	$2,105,600			

Author Note: This report is available to each agent in the MLS. Remember there are many MLS vendors so the information may be displayed differently, but the same information will be present. This report presents an accurate representation of agent production. The key to authentication is the MLS origin.

Figure 2. Agent production report

Remember to Consider the Company, Too

All agents are not equal, nor are the companies they represent. You will find marginal agents at good companies and at marginal companies, and the same for good agents. Some additional questions to ask each agent are these:

> ▶ **If a home buyer asks what a home is worth, what do you say?** You are looking for their familiarity with agency law. It is in the company's best interest to be certain they have

agency choices down pat. If they do not, it says something about the company.

▶ **Do you have price-range preferences or particular areas in which you are most proficient?** You are testing for consistency. Check against their references, or, at a different point in the interview, ask for their MLS production record for the last twelve months that reveals the locations of the production. You want someone familiar with properties and the community in your area.

▶ **Do you have an assistant or assistants?** You are seeking to understand how the agent works, but some companies offer legal or secretarial assistance with document preparation. There are other ways the company may help to free up the agent's time to interact with customers and clients.

▶ **Can you add anything you feel would help assure your selection?** Most will have other information to add, and you get a sense about them as a person. Do they mention the company here without prompting?

▶ **What is your favorite customer service "Wow" story?** How did the client benefit from it? An answer like, "I have too many to count," is not a real answer.

Asking follow-up questions offers you a chance to observe them in action. It also inspires meaningful dialogue. My hope at DearMonty.com is that the information in this guide will be helpful to you in developing the most important follow-up questions.

Select an agent and the company that has the knowledge, skill, and services to assist you in saving time and money. Select the person who best provides his or her time, quality answers, and data you need to make informed decisions with confidence.

It should take a sincere willingness to serve, a high level of competency, and good company support to become your agent. The answers should be right for your situation and "tested" during your selection process. Trust, but verify. A promise made during a conversation requiring agent follow-up should be noted, reminding you to verify that the follow-up occurred. No follow-up is a harbinger of things to come. Your efforts here will help you select with confidence.

Your goal is to select the company and the agent that have the knowledge and services to assist you with efficient, honest, and informed service. Consider the agents who have a supportive broker or manager behind them, which you hear about in some of their answers. A good company does not mean the biggest company, or the smallest company, or the company that spends the most money on advertising. It means an actual customer focus around information, transparency, and agreed-upon communication levels—and, in the end, results.

Now that you have interviewed three agents, asked questions, and took notes, you're ready to choose an agent. If one doesn't shine, eliminate that person. It has been my experience that one or more will shine. The best possible scenario for you is that they *all* shine. You choose the one you feel the best about, based on their actions and the quality and sincerity of their answers. Comparing their answers can be very telling.

If you are selling, your decision will lead to asking your agent of choice to submit a draft listing agreement for your review, create a selling strategy based on market activity, and discuss the future communication instrument (cell phone, text, or phone call) and frequency or cause of your future interaction together.

If you are looking to buy a home, set expectations together at the front end about how you will communicate together, and set a plan for finding the right home and your viewing requirements.

3

UNDERSTANDING THE MARKETPLACE

A
S YOU ARE INTERVIEWING the agents, the real estate market is the second factor to examine. Knowing the market will often affect a number of your important decisions. Often, consumers will meet agents when they are out investigating neighborhoods. There is no time limit or requirement to bunch the interviews. Some people will conduct three interviews in one day; others could take over a month. It depends on your circumstances and motivation. Just don't stop until you get to three.

The key source of the information you will need comes through the real estate agents you speak with as you begin your agent search and as you seek information about different neighborhoods to live in as a buyer, or what the market is like in your neighborhood as a seller. Attending open houses is one of the best methods to accomplish these tasks simultaneously; the first is gathering information about competing homes in terms of understanding value, and second is observing real estate agents at work, gathering information from them about the market, and considering whether they may be an agent for you to interview.

What are other sources to pick up information about neighborhoods, schools, and the pulse of the neighborhood besides from real estate agents? People-in-the-know include title company employees, mortgage lenders, teachers, mail carriers, and home inspectors, who may also have an opinion as to market conditions.

These tasks are easier than they seem because you want to shop for these services as well as for your agent. For example, shopping for a mortgage consists of talking to multiple loan originators. Loan originators are people who sell mortgage products. Banks, credit unions, mortgage brokers, and online lenders are examples of companies that offer mortgages. When you are sorting them out, a valuable way to get other opinions about the market or other suppliers is to interject side questions. "What do you think of the Paisley Park neighborhood?" "Have you had any experience you could share about Betsy Brown at Smart Realty?" "Do you like the Bay School District?"

If you are a potential home buyer, a practical method when beginning your home search (you do this after you have been preapproved for a mortgage loan) is to ask an agent to show you a home with your required features currently for sale in several different neighborhoods. It is possible that some of the features you are seeking will be available in some neighborhoods but not in others. In the corporate-relocation world, viewing these "representative samples" is called an "area tour." Taking some extra time up front, early in your search, can often help you reduce your search time and, if necessary, adjust your requirements accordingly. It often can reduce the time it takes to locate your perfect home.

Vendors are in the market every day. You are in the market only a few times in your life. They are a treasure trove of information that can be helpful to you.

What Information Is Important?

A few key pieces of information will help you understand the market in which you live:

The law of supply and demand: By considering the number of competing properties compared to the sales rate, you can get an idea of the current balance between supply and demand. Here Dear Monty is talking about the market *in your price range*. Many markets have stagnant price ranges while other price points are sizzling, so be mindful of this fact when seeking to understand the market. For example, if there are sixty competing properties in the submarket you want to live in and forty-two sales of similarly priced homes in the price range you are aiming for in the past six months, it suggests a seller's market. If there were only four comparable sales, a buyer's market is evident. In the former market segment, a seller would have the upper hand because the demand is evident, and buyers may have little power to negotiate, as they will be competing with other buyers. In the latter market segment, the buyer would have the upper hand to negotiate aggressively with only four comparable sales.

This means that the strategies of both buyer and seller will change depending on the condition of a market. Here are examples for a seller and a buyer:

A seller in a strong seller's market may try to start an auction sale by not reacting to offers that are submitted before a certain date. In a buyer's market, that same seller may price at the low end of the home's value range to attempt to attract the few potential buyers and be the first home to sell by eliminating the neighboring competition.

A buyer in a strong seller's market may attempt to make their offer for a home more desirable. Offering more than the list price, submitting a preapproval letter with the offer (a preapproval is much stronger than a prequalification letter), sending along a note, or proceeding without a home-inspection contingency are all tactics that can sometimes influence a home seller. If a buyer's market is apparent, buyers will make lower offers, negotiate for other concessions (like furniture), shop other houses simultaneously, and even ask for new carpeting or appliance-replacement credits.

Fluctuations in interest rates: While timing your purchase or sale around interest rates is fairly common, many people do not have the luxury to consider interest rates when they are buying or selling a home. As an example, when a job relocation is offered, the employee will not think much about interest rates. For those buyers who are concerned with interest rates because their payments are affected, waiting for interest rates to fall may not reap any extra benefit. Declining interest rates can bring both new buyers and sellers into the market, and if the buyers outweigh the sellers, home prices can escalate, which could wipe out any interest rate savings to a home buyer.

Conversely, rising interest rates on mortgages can slow the sales rate and contribute to an oversupply of inventory (more homes are for sale), which softens prices (desperate sellers take lower prices). Waiting for interest rate fluctuations may not deliver the intended result.

Submarket statistics: Sellers and buyers should be aware of the average length of time it currently takes to sell a home in their price range; buyers may want to compare current data with those of the last two years. The average market length can be another indication of a seller's market or buyer's market. Also, keep in mind that the concept of "average" may differ from property to property. Many markets have climates that can have an effect on sales. Hot weather in summer in the Southwest, cold temperatures in the Midwest and Northeast, and monsoons and humidity in the South all can affect real estate activity. While the statistics will show noticeable changes in seasonal activity, many buyers and sellers continue to buy and sell year-round in all markets. How much weather statistics affect the seasonal markets is often misinterpreted.

To illustrate the value of utilizing your real estate agent to provide sub-market data for you, below are the results of a request to an agent for information in a particular neighborhood. The agent was asked to provide the information, but shared that they did not have the MLS skill to produce the map. What I observed with that comment is it is a trait of a honest person. Honesty is the most important attribute you are seeking. He also was able to defeat his lack of computer skills by sharing he had a colleague he worked with when this type of request surfaced.

It is likely the MLS in your area has these same capabilities. The request was to gather data on canceled (Figure 3) and sold listings (Figure 4) in the past 24 months and current listings (Figure 5). The boundaries by street name were furnished to define the exact location. The agent delivered the answers by providing an MLS link to my email inbox within 24 hours. A property data sheet, in addition to the map, was included on each property. According to Figure 5, there are two homes for sale within the requested boundaries. How would you describe this sub-market?

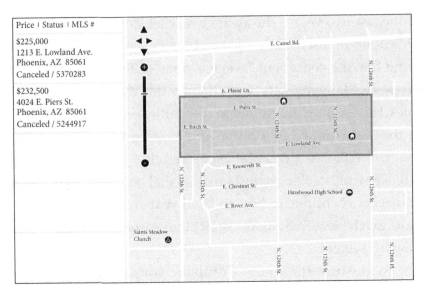

Figure 3. Canceled Listings

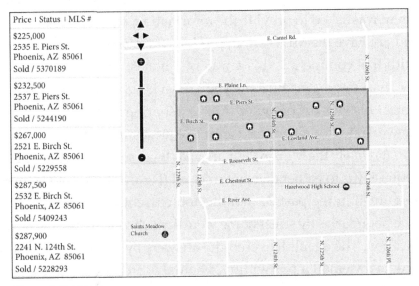

Figure 4. Sold Listings

The best information is obtained from real estate agents who are adept at retrieving a variety of timely statistics from MLS data.

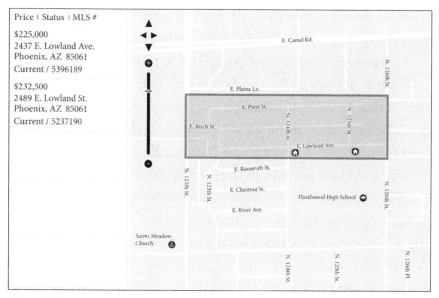

Figure 5. Current Listings

If you are selling, the goal is to project the "sales rate" of homes similar to yours in the coming months. The more sales and listing data you can gather, the more dependable the calculation. Remember to search only your price range and submarket. Do not be surprised if you receive different answers from the agents you talk with. This may be the result of how a particular agent perceives your submarket. Are they using the same geographic boundaries? Are certain areas to be discounted? Is your price range well defined? Here are the questions to ask the agents (they can find the answers for you in the MLS).

- How many homes are currently for sale in our price range?

- How many homes were for sale last year at this point?

- From this point forward last year, how many new listings came onto the market during the next six months?

By assuming that this year will be similar, we can predict X number of new listings in the next six months. Adding the current inventory, less last year's expired listings during that same six-month period, to the predicted new listings, we can predict the total competing inventory.

Applying this same logic to the corresponding time period last year for sold and closed statistics, we can also predict the number of sold and closed homes in the coming six months.

For example, assume eighty similar homes are currently on or coming onto the market, and twenty homes sold last year in the following six months. This information suggests that twenty homes will sell this year in the coming six months. With eighty homes for sale and twenty projected to sell, the projected sales rate will be three or four sales per month, a 25 percent sales rate. The data suggest it will be a buyer's market. Remember that markets are cyclical, and there is no guarantee that history will repeat itself, but this approach is better than a "gut feeling."

With this information in hand, whether you are buying, selling, or both, the potential impact in the future helps you make sound decisions. As a seller, using the previous example, if an offer is submitted on your home, and it is 10 percent off your asking price, you can ask yourself how long you will have to wait for the next offer, and will it be higher than this one? For the buyer who made this offer, what will you do if the seller turns down your offer? Go higher, or keep looking, knowing there are more new listings on the way?

Present and future economic trends: Consider the area's employment outlook, property taxes, and other community factors, such as school district performance. A company layoff or constant property tax increases in a community can negatively affect the market in that area (making it more difficult to sell homes).

Caution: This information applies to the overall market when you are entering the marketplace—before you have isolated a home you are interested in investigating. When you do identify a property, you should undertake a similar investigation into the submarket activity of that property. Typically, there are "markets within markets." Different price ranges, different neighborhoods, and other influences affect the sales rate and property values. Examples of this may be school district performance, distance to a mass transit system, or crime rates. Every community will have its nuances. More about this subject in chapter 4.

At this point in the process, you have likely identified the real estate agent you want to work with, and you have turned her into a resource to gather any market information you did not receive earlier. Believe it or not, while many agents believe they have a good sense of how your submarket is performing, it may not be accurate. Your agent will likely be impressed that you are taking this approach in understanding the market. You may be teaching the agent something new.

Access to the MLS for this type of research is just as important to you as the MLS is as a repository of inventory. I know this because at our relocation company, we often found that real estate agents did not understand why we wanted the identical data we are suggesting will help you. The relocation company we owned managed the home sale of our clients' relocating employees. We used these data regularly to better understand how we should price those homes when we took them into our inventory. We also updated this information when we received an offer, to help decide whether we should counter offer, at what price we should counter offer, or whether we should accept the offer. We always credited this market data exercise as one of the little tricks we used to help achieve the best results for our clients and their employees.

You have now picked up three valuable tools that will aid you immensely as you travel the real estate process. You have the big picture; you learned how to pick your agent; and now you know how to direct your agent to gather certain MLS information to help you make the best decisions. You are now ready to learn how to evaluate a home.

4

HOW TO EVALUATE PROPERTY

REAL ESTATE LAW DEFINES market value as the price a willing seller and a willing buyer— each *fully informed* and neither acting under duress—agree to in a negotiation. Dear Monty believes "fully informed" includes a minimal understanding of the real estate appraisal process. For most of us, these are the primary considerations:

- The sale price of comparable properties that have sold recently

- The list price of comparable properties that are currently on the market

- The property's relative condition, quality, age, location, and other features

- The replacement cost of the property if replicated on a comparable site

 ▶ General real estate conditions in the applicable
   neighborhood

One of the biggest misconceptions in real estate is that every
home "has its price." Taken literally, it suggests that every buyer
will reach the same conclusion on a home's value. This belief is
simply not true. Even appraisers, who have extensive training to
evaluate homes, will not agree on a home's value. If you paid ten
appraisers to determine the price of the same home on the same day,
each opinion would be different. Let me show you. See Figure 6.

In Figure 6, appraisals would be reviewed first to determine
what comparables or calculations were driving the appraisers'
opinions. Is their math accurate? Did they miss a feature adjustment? How old are the sales? Were the comparables all arm's-length
transactions? Are the comparables in similar neighborhoods
and developments? Are the comparables the best comparables?
Through a process of sifting and winnowing the appraisals that
are error-free and that exhibited sound judgment in feature
adjustments, the best comparables can be identified to zoom in
on a tighter range of value. For example, one common method to
tighten the range of value is to automatically discard the highest
and the lowest opinions. Appraisal 1 and appraisal 10 would be
eliminated in Figure 6 on the next page.

We often struggle through difficult negotiations to reach
agreement on price when there is more than one right price. The
real truth is that every home has its price *range*. The two major
influences on this range of value is the number of relevant comparable sales and activity in the marketplace. As actual comparable
sales diminish, the range of value widens. When there is little
market activity, the range of value widens. The range of value is

what is a home really worth?

10 certified appraisers • same house • same day

Figure 6. What is a home really worth? The illustration depicts the results if ten appraisers were asked to evaluate the same home on the same day. So what is this home really worth now?

best expressed with the highest price you *could* expect and the lowest price you *should* expect, based on several independent, well-reasoned opinions. Your goal is to assure yourself that you are within that range of value.

If you are selling, your three finalist agents will each provide an opinion about your home's range of value. As each opinion will be different, between the thinking and judgment of the three agents and your newfound appraisal knowledge, you will be in an enviable position to make an informed judgment on your home's range of value.

If you are buying and you have collected data sheets and taken notes on the homes you have seen in private showings or open houses, you already have timely, helpful information. If you are a customer, the agent showing the home can furnish you with additional sales that he views as comparable, but he likely cannot give you his opinion of value. If you have a buyer agent, she can render her opinion. Is it a reliable opinion? The only way you can truly judge is to understand how an appraisal or opinion of value is created.

It is common for people to buy and sell homes without the benefit of knowing how to review an appraisal or broker price opinion (BPO). They will make judgments on "gut feel," their agent's "gut feel," or by using comparable sales that often are not good comparables. With the advent of the Internet, some home buyers and home sellers actually depend on online appraisals. It is unwise to depend on a computer. You are well advised to know how to evaluate a home before any negotiation begins. The key here is the phrase, "before any negotiation begins."

In addition to your investigation and efforts, there are resources available to assist in determining a home's range of value. The two common resources used by buyers and sellers are the "broker price opinion" (BPO), and an independent appraisal by a fee appraiser.

The Broker Price Opinion (BPO)

Also known as a competitive market analysis (CMA), a properly completed BPO or CMA will examine and report on all five of the considerations listed early in this chapter (the sale price of comparable properties, homes currently on the market in this area, condition of the property, replacement cost, and general conditions of the neighborhood). There is no real difference between the BPO and the CMA.

Your agent will gather and analyze the information, render an opinion of value for a particular home, and present this information in the form of a written document. You should look at the features of the comparable properties and be prepared to question the agent's analysis and judgment. While an agent's familiarity with the current market conditions and individual properties lends credibility to his or her opinion, they remain just opinions. A BPO properly prepared by an agent using appraisal methodology can provide a reasonable home value range. Your agent should be ready and willing to discuss all aspects of his or her findings.

The Fee Appraisal

Properties are appraised for various reasons such as setting a fair market value, establishing a value for an estate when the owner dies, determining how much to insure the property for, setting conditions for condemnations, and for establishing a value for mortgage loan purposes for a lender. The more detail the report requires, the more it will cost to develop.

Costs for appraisals can range from $150 to $5,000 and more, depending on the geographic market, the type of appraisal you require, the type and complexity of the property, and the credentials

of the appraiser. The appraiser will analyze the same five considerations previously identified, and if comparable rental homes are
available, he or she may also elect to include that information.

When reviewing an appraisal or broker price opinion, be
prepared to question the validity of the comparable properties
and the person's analysis and judgment. Dear Monty recommends
attending open houses, talking with agents, and gathering data
sheets to take notes on. This is the reason you have been engaging
in the exercise. It is a mistake to accept the appraiser's opinion
without taking the time to examine and understand it.

ASK MONTY

Melinda Asks: Is the seller of a home privy to the appraisal
value of the home that the buyer paid for? Does the agent
representing the buyer have that information, or is the agent
privy to it? Who is entitled to the information or can access
it? Is the agent or his company in a position to assist the seller
in obtaining the information if the buyer is not willing to
share it? What if the appraisal is significantly higher than
the listing price? What are the financial ramifications if we
decide to back out? We think the appraisal came in higher,
and we would keep it as an investment and rent it out.

Dear Monty Advises: Melinda, there is much information
that is not included in your question that may impact my
response, so these comments are qualified and general in
nature. While it is certainly true that the appraisal may
have exceeded the purchase price, there are a number of
other possibilities that are equally as plausible.

Every state has real estate laws that vary. Many states have pre-drafted, fill-in-the-blank forms for uniformity, but not all states. Unless the purchase contract states the buyer must share the appraisal results, the buyer may not be required to share. You need to consult a local attorney to review your contract and the law to render an opinion on the appraisal sharing requirement, if there is one. At that same appointment, also ask the attorney about the ramifications were you to break the contract.

- On the financing side of purchase contracts, many buyers simply do not have an obligation or a willingness to share much information from a privacy point of view. Privacy could be the reason the buyer has apparently refused your request.

- Another reason could be that the buyer has yet to convince the lender to make the loan or negotiated the rate and terms. It is possible the reason for this be that the appraisal came in low.

- It is possible that the buyer has negotiated some type of portfolio loan that is not sold to Freddie Mac or Fannie Mae and that neither party wants to discuss the arrangement.

- It is very possible that the buyer's agent does not know the amount of the appraisal.

It has been my experience in real estate that out-of-state property owners with little or no property-management training or experience are unhappy with being a landlord.

There are people today who know the law very well and take advantage. Little or no rent, raising the ire of the neighbors, or literally destroying the property while they are living in the house is common.

On the other hand, your background and training may blend well with the prospect of becoming a landlord, if your attorney signs off on your ability to terminate the contract.

Without the benefit of the important history, this is the best I can do. Also consider that there is a financing contingency you agreed to when you entered into the contract. Get legal advice, and proceed carefully.

The Difference Between the Fee Appraisal and the BPO

There are some differences between a fee appraisal and a BPO. While law requires neither of these documents when you sell a home, the appraisal is required if there is a lender involved when you buy a home. The main differences are these:

- The fee appraiser specializes in appraising property rather than selling the property; the appraiser has no conflict of interest, and someone pays the appraiser for his or her opinion. The fee appraiser's standards of practice obligate the appraiser to physically inspect the property to be appraised (called the subject property) and drive by the comparable sales. Each state dictates the education required for securing each type of appraisal license and the continuing-education credits to maintain it.

‣ The BPO, on the other hand, is a free opinion developed by your agent, who has access to much of the same information as the appraiser but does have a self-interest in any sale. The BPO may contain comparable properties the agent has not seen or physically driven past. The BPO is free to a homeowner looking for an opinion of fair market value. The real estate agent must physically inspect the property before rendering an opinion. There is no prelicense education or continuing-education credit required for providing a free BPO to consumers.

Another factor to consider is the purpose of the fee appraisal. Is the objective to give you guidance on what to offer for the home? Or is it for the lender to confirm the loan they are contemplating is secure? Or are you engaging in an appraisal to determine at what price you should list the property for sale?

The appraiser is responsible to the party that engages the appraiser, regardless of who pays for the appraisal. For example, when you pay for the appraisal included in your mortgage loan closing costs, the lender ordered the appraisal. Therefore, in the case of home mortgage loans, the appraiser is working for the lender. An agent BPO is for the express purpose of offering an opinion of the property's fair market value to the home seller or to provide a written opinion of value to a potential home buyer who has entered into a buyer agency agreement. A home buyer who chooses not to enter a buyer agency agreement becomes a customer and does not receive an opinion of value but can look at a number of comparable home sales to make their comparisons.

A Misconception

Another common real estate value misconception is that the municipal property assessment can be used as a reasonable indicator of fair market value. The municipal property assessment is for the purpose of taxation and is not intended to be an opinion of current market value. Property rarely sells for the assessed valuation. It is either more or less, and it can be significantly more or less. View it as the least-reliable source of value information.

The Property Inspection

You may immediately wonder why the home inspection is being discussed in the evaluation section of this book. It is because the home inspection's purpose is to determine the condition of a home. A home's condition is one of the primary considerations in determining value.

When you decide to have a home inspection, the major components of the home will be visually inspected and, in some cases, tested by a trained professional. You will receive a written report outlining details about the home and the inspection results. Components inspected generally include the roof, heating units, plumbing, electrical system, structure, foundation, major appliances, and much more.

Dear Monty advocates that sellers have their homes inspected before listing the home for sale in most instances. In the absence of a home inspection from the seller, a home buyer should consider a home inspection before submitting an offer. Prediction: Many real estate agents will advise against this request. Why? The agent may see the inspection before the offer as a potential roadblock to a successful negotiation. They prefer to set the price and then negotiate over inspection issues. You alone will make the decision on how to proceed with the right to cure (explained soon) based on your motivation, your knowledge of evaluating a property, the seller's circumstances, and the current status of the market in the neighborhood.

What an Inspection Is Not

The purpose of the home inspection is to discover and disclose the condition of the principal structural and mechanical components of the home. Because this is a visual examination, an inspection does have limitations. The inspection is not

- A code compliance or safety inspection

- A valuation of the premises

- A detailed report of minor defects

- A representation of whether a buyer should purchase the home

- A warranty

Keep in mind that an inspection is made as of a particular date. It is possible that the condition could change after that point in time.

The Right-to-Cure Provision

Many states have some statute or administrative rules regarding home inspections, which may be included in a preprinted offer-to-purchase form. If the law provides the seller the default right to cure any defects discovered in a home inspection, you should consider an inspection before you submit an offer or negotiate the right-to-cure provision from your offer. In some states, the buyer cannot rescind the contract if defects are found and the seller agrees to repair or replace. In other states, the buyer can rescind the contract after inspection at will. As an example, the offer-to-purchase form in Wisconsin allows the buyer to chose between allowing the seller the right-to-cure, or not allowing the right-to-cure. Here is the URL to the flow chart, www.wra.org/InspectionFlowchart, that demonstrates each right-to-cure step in Wisconsin. Make certain you understand how the right-to-cure provision works in your state.

Once the price is set between the buyer and seller, the negotiation shifts to the repair or replacement of the home's components. If the buyer had known of the need for a repair or replacement before the price was set, would the buyer have made the same offer? It is Dear Monty's opinion the buyer should control the repairs or replacements, because when the seller has the right, there is often dissatisfaction. The following Q&A answers a home-inspection question to provide a home buyer's perspective.

ASK MONTY

Jeri and Judy Ask: We are looking at a sixty-year-old home. It seems to have good bones, but I see several red flags. Is there any advantage to having a pre-offer inspection completed before we make an offer?

Dear Monty's Answer: A home inspection is a necessary component in the purchase of any home. Although less likely, flaws or errors can and do occur even in brand-new homes. Even quality contractors make mistakes. Whether a home is a hundred years old or brand new, a home inspection is a valuable service.

There are multiple circumstances in every transaction that could impact the direction one takes in making a decision on a pre-offer inspection. Here are the primary advantages and disadvantages of having a home inspection before making an offer:

Advantages

- You may discover issues that will cause you not to move forward.

- If you do make an offer, it does not have to contain an inspection contingency.

- You have better factual information before you decide an offering price.

- If you do not make an offer, you may avoid other costs triggered by the contract.

Disadvantages

- With no contract, there is a chance the seller may sell to another buyer.

- You still may not be able to come to terms with the seller.

A pre-offer inspection is not a factor to introduce in every circumstance. It should be considered only after reviewing certain data and only after you have determined you want the house.

Pre-offer Considerations

Can you find a good home inspector? Just as not all home builders and real estate agents are equal, so goes the home inspector.
Regardless of the timing of the inspection, when you order a home
inspection, consider researching the options and making a judgment on which inspector to engage, based on your research. If
you take a recommendation from a real estate agent, make certain
they provide at least three names. Research each one, including
the agent's favorite.

Consider interviewing three inspectors. Just as one would interview multiple agents, contractors, and other service providers,
review their websites, call a couple of their references, review
their qualifications and experience, review their contract and
deliverables (a sample inspection), and ask them questions about
promises in their offering or promotion. A good way to ask your
questions is by email. Good inspectors are busy during daylight
hours, and they will respond after sunset, which dictates the
termination of physical inspections (never hire a home inspector
who does inspections at night). Make certain they understand
the pre-offer situation.

Inspection companies have different offerings. Does the inspection company re-inspect at a preclosing walk-through for a smaller
fee? Many inspectors offer some guarantee. For example, an inspection company may claim that, if they make a mistake, they will
buy the house from you for what you paid. See that the inspectors'
promotions and promises line up with your needs.

Understand the market conditions in the neighborhood. If homes are going pending in a very short period, the pre-offer inspection may not be appealing to the seller, or they may find another buyer before you can act on the results. The home's length of time on the market, along with how long it will take the inspector to deliver the report, is useful in determining the logic of a pre-offer inspection. If the statistics suggest the home may be on the market a month or two, or it has been on the market for some time, the odds to use the pre-inspection to make better valuation decisions increase.

Will the seller agree to order the inspection? Dear Monty recommends most sellers have their home pre-inspected and correct any issues before they list their home. A property owner who takes this step is wise. It matters not who purchases the inspection. What is important is the report's accuracy. Utilized correctly, a proper home inspection also serves as a marketing tool.

Why few buyers order prepurchase inspections. Many real estate agents will discourage the idea of seller pre-inspections or a buyer asking for a pre-offer inspection. This pushback could come from either agent. The agent fears blame if a contract never materializes. Also, the agent may fear it will "kill the deal" and see the pre-offer inspection as more risk in their time investment in a client.

 ASK MONTY ▬▬▬▬▬▬▬▬▬▬▬▬▬▬▬▬▬▬▬▬

Hannah Asks: Monty, we paid $400+ for a home inspection. We were living out of state, but both the Realtor and a friend of ours accompanied the inspector. The owner did not have the water running, and there were many issues with the electrical. The owner assured our representatives that they would fix these problems. There was little more than a note in the actual report.

After closing, we found some glaring issues that, had they appeared in the inspector's report, would have led us not to purchase the home. While we have been able to use the home warranty for particular issues, there are others (an improperly installed shower) that were not covered and will cost us several hundred dollars. What recourse do we have?

Dear Monty's Answer: Hello, Hannah, and thanks for your question. If these issues can be repaired or replaced for "several hundred dollars," it may not be worth your time to pursue it any further. Perhaps you should chalk the loss up to experience, make the repairs, and move forward.

The inspector may have "errors and omissions" insurance or an inspection warranty that will cover the losses. The inspector may also be willing to negotiate some settlement. Most inspectors will limit their exposure by either rescheduling the inspection when the water system is functioning or inspecting the home with a noticeable disclosure in the report that they did not check the plumbing system because the system was shut off.

I have not seen the report, but it is also possible that the home inspector was not competent. The water system not being operative is a huge red flag. Did you hire the inspector? How did you find the inspector? Did your Realtor throw out any cautionary flags? Bring this situation to the inspector's attention to hear what they have to say.

Knowing that the water was not operational at inspection and that the inspection revealed electrical issues, why did you not insist on a pre-closing walk-through? Delegating the responsibility to a friend is usually not a good idea because they do not know how to react in a situation like this; all they can do is report it to you. An owner promising to fix problems before closing is notorious in the real estate business as a potential post-closing problem. While some home sellers do it right, many will utilize inferior parts, have poor workmanship, or, worse yet, neglect to perform.

It occurs to me that you bear some responsibility in this situation.

Valuing a Home When Selling or Buying

The best information on a home's value comes from knowledge-able people who have done the research and documented their results. Individual perceptions and hearsay without facts cause confusion and misrepresentation. Analyzing the five considerations of a real estate appraisal is when you gain a real understanding of a home's range of value.

An excellent way to gather home-value information before you list your home or buy a home is to attend open houses at similar properties in the neighborhood. The time and energy you invest in each home you view in your search become a part of your experience. A side benefit of this activity is observing agents at work. Gathering relevant specifications from each open house will help you determine if the home being shown is a likely comparable to your home if you are selling. As a buyer, the open houses add data to your evaluation quiver to be drawn upon when you are evaluating a particular home. This information will add confidence to your review of the experts' opinions when you are evaluating their work.

Do not leave the task of setting a home's range of value entirely to the agents or appraisers. Why? Because neither the real estate appraiser nor your agent will be writing out a check for the purchase price, so don't abdicate to them the full responsibility for valuing and pricing your home. While home sellers do review an appraisal report or the agent's BPO, there is often little or no time spent educating them on how the conclusions about value were reached. Further, there is often no explanation of the rationale for the adjustments made between your property and comparable properties. The appraiser's decisions can affect the range of value by 10 to 30 percent. The same can be said for a home buyer, who typically does not see an appraisal until after they have committed to purchase a home.

Most buyers and sellers do not understand the appraisal process well. Consequently, in my experience, they are not aware of the critical questions to ask. This dependency on the agent's BPO or the home appraisal is indeed understandable. After all, you think, because the state grants a real estate agent a license to conduct business, he or she should have the best idea of local values. It may surprise you to learn that, in Wisconsin, prelicense training and continuing-education requirements for real estate agents contain virtually no education on appraisal methodology. The state abdicates this responsibility to the real estate industry, the bulk of whose training is about how to find and convert prospects. Dear Monty suspects most other states take a similar position. Assuming all the verifiable information about the home is documented, it is the choice of comparables and the resulting value adjustments that make the most difference in the derived value estimates.

Last, consider that an appraisal report is just one experienced person's opinion of value. Having just one opinion in the atmosphere you just became aware of is a significant reason a home seller should interview multiple agents, and an important reason to become familiar with the key elements of an appraisal document.

The Power to Protect Your Investment

Dear Monty is advising you to dig deeper into understanding property evaluation. Sad to say, but understanding this information can make you better informed than many real estate agents. Also, knowing how to use this information will help you make confident negotiating decisions and may save you many thousands of dollars.

Dear Monty received a phone call last year from a home seller who thanked us for saving her money. She had an agent complete a BPO and was ready to list before she read Dear Monty's advice about how to choose a real estate agent. After reading the suggestion about speaking with three agents, she asked another agent for an opinion, which was much higher and well justified. She decided to use the new agent, and that agent's opinion turned out to be correct. It was $50,000 higher than her first agent's opinion.

You might be asking yourself if a BPO is one of the services you are paying for, when you hire an agent. Yes, it is. However, Dear Monty is talking about your largest single financial investment. We also know that the opinions of experts vary, often significantly, on the same property. The idea of educating yourself to protect your interests is logical. The more you know about how to evaluate a home, the better prepared you will be when it comes time to buy or sell one. Here are your benefits:

- Gain confidence in your decisions.

- Know how to ask the agent or appraiser the right questions.

- Become a better negotiator with better information.

- Know what information to ask your agent to retrieve from the MLS.

ASK MONTY

Sandra and Don Ask: We are thinking of selling our home. We ordered a home appraisal, which we just received in the mail. We do not agree with the opinion of value they came up with, but we do not know how to go about challenging them. What should we do?

Dear Monty's Answer: For you to question the appraiser successfully, you will have to demonstrate a substantial reason to convince them to reconsider. You paid them for their opinion. To reach a conclusion, the appraiser has a duty to verify all of the information assembled in the document. It is relatively easy to correct the error when the appraiser did not account for all of the home's square footage or missed an outbuilding. It may be harder to convince them to make a change when their documentation is correct and the conclusion is causing the disagreement.

Why Are There Three Approaches to Value?

There are multiple approaches to determining value. While each method brings perspective to a home's value, each method also has limitations. Blending the three methods allows the preparer to consider multiple viewpoints in reaching a conclusion. The three approaches are the cost approach, the income approach, and the market-data approach. The most likely place for error is either the choice of comparables or the adjustment calculations for the differences between the features of your home (the subject property) and the comparables in the market-data approach section.

In the appraisal document, you will find a comparable sales grid. The grid identifies the chosen comparables across the page, and the adjustments the appraiser calculated for each feature are in columns under each comparable.

Check The Comparable Sales

Double-check the items on this list for your home (subject-property column) to verify that the information is correct. For example, square-footage calculations can be a source of error because homes can be tricky to measure. In our relocation business, where we had two or three appraisals on every home, it was not unusual to see differences in square-footage calculations—and occasionally considerable differences.

Check the Individual Feature Adjustments

Where there are calculable differences, the appraiser adjusts the features considered between the comparable sales and the subject property. They never alter the subject, only the comparables. Not all features will require change. Sometimes the compared feature shows the comparable is less valuable than the subject.

Sometimes the feature in the comparable is more valuable than the feature in the subject. The formula for adjusting comparables is to add (+) if the subject is better and subtract

(–) if the subject is lesser. The tabulation of the additions and subtractions are at the bottom of the grid.

The Last Step

If the total adjustments after the additions and subtractions net out to be more than $30,000, on a $175,000 home, these are likely not the best comparables. As a home's value rises, the individual adjustments may increase with that value.

The appraiser driving by the comparables adds considerable value to deciding which properties are the best choices. You can learn a lot driving by the comparables yourself. The comparables homes should be in neighborhoods similar to yours. It will be difficult to persuade an appraiser to change his or her opinion, lacking the discovery of incorrect math calculations, observations, or significant deficiencies in the choice of comparables and adjustments.

Know the Three Methods of Determining a Home's Value

There are multiple ways to determine value. While each method brings perspective to a home's value, each method also has limitations. Blending the three methods allows the preparer to consider multiple viewpoints in reaching a conclusion. The three approaches and their strengths and constraints are as follows:

- **Cost of replacement approach:** When evaluating a home, always remember that cost of replacement sets the upper limit of value. What would it cost to build? The main limitation of the cost approach is that it deals only with the cost of replacing the home new, less depreciation, in the marketplace.

▶ **Income approach:** All improved real estate has economic value. There are two choices for property owners: occupy (live in your own home) or rent (find someone to pay monthly rent to live in your home). When property can produce income, that income determines rates of return on capital invested. The marketplace dictates the rents based on supply and demand. It is a serious question to ask. How much rent could the home generate? The limitation of this method is that often there is little or no rental market where you want to live. Leases are not recorded, so finding comparable rents is hard.

▶ **Market approach:** The law of supply and demand is the driving force here. What are similar homes selling for in the neighborhood? How many similar homes are currently for sale? How often does one of these homes sell? The market approach is the primary approach to value in single-family homes today.

The Origin of the Data

The MLS data sheet is the source of the critical information necessary to determine the acceptability of the best comparable sales available. These data sheets are emailed to you by an agent during the interview process, handed out at open houses, and used to generate company fliers for disseminating information about the property.

Keep these data sheets in a folder, as they are the key to evaluating the comparable sales agents will present to you to add credence to his or her opinion. Below in Figure 7, is an MLS data sheet. Keep in mind that selecting a comparable is a subjective exercise because every home is unique. Driving to the comparable homes to see them with your own eyes provides you an advantage over a person who did not take the time. With a bit of practice, one can become skilled in choosing the best comparable homes.

2364 RIVERSIDE DR   Village of Allouez, WI 543131946

List: $399,000

Finished Bedrooms 5	Finished Full Baths: 3	Finished Half Baths: 0		
Style/Building Type:	Quad-Level		1st Fl. M-Bed:	No
County:	Brown		Bath off M-Bed:	Yes
Subdivision:			Split Bedroom:	No
City:	GREEN BAY		Frml Dining Rm:	Yes
School District:	Green Bay Area		1st Fl Laundry:	No
Net Taxes*/Tax Year:	$6,036/16		2nd Fl Laundry:	No
Prop. Tax ID:	AL-1517		Fireplace:	Yes
Plat Sect. #:				
Age:	51-74 YEARS		Central Air:	Yes
Garage #1:	Detatched/2.5 Car (min width 24')/		Home Warranty:	No
Garage #2:	None/ /		Rests. Convenant:	Unknown
Walk-out:	Yes		Floor Plain:	Unknown
			HOA YN/Fee/Type:	/$/

Photo Credit: Pete Seroogy

Photo Credit: Pete Seroogy - Green Bay Home Tour

FEATURES

Exterior Finish:	Aluminium/Steel	Water:	Public
Water Heater:	Gas	Waste:	Sewer
Heat Fuel Type:	Gas	Seller Financing:	None
Heat/Cooling:	Hot Water	Zoning:	Residential
Gar. Ext./Misc:	Door Opener	Lot Desc:	Sloping, Landscaped, Shade
Bsmt/Lwr. Lvl:	Walkout Entrance (Door)	Fireplace:	Trees
Foundation:	Block	Outbuildings:	Wood Burn. Fireplace
Driveway:	Black Top	Gas/Electric:	None
Misc. Exterior Incl:		Other Water:	220 Range Hookup, 220
Misc. Interior Incl:	Smoke Alarm	Architecture:	Dryer Hookup
Appliances Incl:	Oven/Range-Elec., Refriger-	Condo Building:	None
Floor Treatment:	ator, Dishwasher	Condo Living Space:	Other
Streets:	Vinyl	Condo Unit Lvl:	
Licensee Inter.:	Public	Condo Misc.:	

Description	Data	Source of Data	Description	Data	Source of Data	Prop. Sub-Type	
Apx. TFA SF (Pre 2007)			Lot, Ftg/SF (Pre 2007):			Waterfron:	Yes
Est. Fin. Above Grade SqFt:	1630	Other - See Remarks	Water Frontage:	162	Assessor/Public Record	New Const:	No
Est. Fin. Below Grade SqFt:	1339	Other - See Remarks	Est. Acreage:	.726	Assessor/Public Record	Farm:	No
Est. Total Abv/Blw Grade:	2969	Other - See Remarks	Est. Lot Size:	X		Condominium:	No
Est. Tot. SqFt. Lot:	31630	Assessor/Public Record	Lot info:			Zero Lot Line:	No
						Propsd Condo	No
Body of Water:	FOX RIVER		Condo Docs:		Ad Code:		
Body of Water Type:	River		Asse/Condo Fees:	$	Zero Lot Line Man/Maint. Doc:		
Est. Water Frontage:	162		Developer Name:		Zero Lot Line Type:		
Src. of Frontage Data:	Assessor/Public Record		Condo Name:		Elem. School:		
Builder Name:			Condo Start Date:		Middle School:		
New Const. Compl:			Condo Compl Date:		High School:		
Est. Compl. Data:			# Units in Condo Dev:				

	DIM	LVL		DIM	LVL	RM TYPE		DIM	LVL
Living Rm	19X15	Main	Other Rm 1	3X5	Main	Foyer/Vestibule	MCR 1	15X14	Lower
Great Rm			Other Rm 2	19X21	Lower	Rec Room	Bdrm 2	11X11	Lower
Family Rm	11X23	Lower	Other Rm 3				Bdrm 3	13X11	Main
Dining Rm - Frml	11X13	Main	Other Rm 4				Bdrm 4	12X11	Upper
Kitchen	11X10	Main					Bdrm 5	10X13	Upper
Dining Area	11X10	Main	Bath 1	Full	Upper		Bath 2	Full	Lower
Laund/Utly Rm			Bath 3	Full	Lower		Bath 4		
Directions	Monroe South to Riverside Dr in Allouez								
Remarks	Waterfront! Sprawling 5 bdrm, 3 bath on river w/tons of updates throughout! Spacious living rm w/gorgeous river views. Formal living & dining rms, family rm w/FP. Msty bdrm w/updated bath. Walk out LL suite w/bdrm, living area, wet bar, refrigerator. Extra slab for parking goes								

Figure 7. MLS Data Sheet

How to Pick Suitable Comparable Sales

No two homes are exactly alike. In valuing a home, the key is to select the sold homes out of the comparable pile that most resemble the subject property. Here are the key features to consider:

- The property's relative condition, quality, age, location, and other features

- General real estate conditions in the applicable neighborhood

- Extent and age of any updating

- Properties that are the same style (ranch, two-story, split level, raised ranch)

- Approximately the same size ground-floor square footage

- About the same age, except if there has been a major remodel

- Same number of baths and half baths

- Same number of bedrooms

- Same room count overall

- Same type and size of garage (attached, unattached, number of stalls)

Below is the first page of search results in a municipality where the query was for *all* sales for six months by ascending price. There were a total of eight pages of results. Many MLS's divide the the geographical territory in their domain into smaller subsets. You have to request the data to drill down to this level. This report provides you with unfiltered data that helps enable you to obtain an understanding of the sub-market in this municipality. This report allows you to view the comparable sales that the appraiser or the agent did not select as a comparable. A change in even one comparable can make a big difference in the value outcome. For you, the buyer or seller, this is where you should seek to understand why one comparable was chosen over another.

ML#	Address	List Price	Sell Price	Firm #	Agent #	Sell Date	Muni
R63926749C	123 6th St.	$187,000	$188,000	1789	836594	06/03/2016	RIDGE
R63910687C	71 Pilgrim Ave	$192,000	$190,000	6308	170177	03/03/2016	RIDGE
R93487719C	70 Bowman St.	$195,000	$195,000	5609	106492	04/15/2016	RIDGE
R93998267C	4 Goldfield Rd.	$200,000	$195,000	1668	743459	03/31/2016	RIDGE
R17485666C	44 Shirley Ave.	$215,000	$225,000	9677	239488	01/29/2016	RIDGE
R92046728C	514 S. Magnolia	$222,000	$200,000	6209	174973	05/06/2016	RIDGE
R56710017C	72 Saxton Ln.	$230,000	$230,000	0564	712492	03/15/2016	RIDGE
R57836567C	7898 Pierce Rd.	$235,000	$245,000	7465	412791	06/24/2016	RIDGE
R01746602C	80 N. Greenrose	$239,000	$239,000	1285	249290	03/31/2016	RIDGE
R17892687C	8044 Parker	$243,000	$243,000	1920	229833	06/02/2016	RIDGE
R09101565C	514 Bohemia	$250,000	$235,000	1765	12309	02/25/2016	RIDGE
R64890111C	101 Arlington	$262,000	$270,000	9520	249881	05/23/2016	RIDGE
R66100272C	739 Meadow St.	$265,000	$270,000	4571	120239	04/29/2016	RIDGE
R93620177C	8751 Thatcher	$269,000	$260,000	1086	349822	04/26/2016	RIDGE
R72037198C	66 Carriage St.	$271,000	$271,000	3948	519346	03/11/2016	RIDGE
R28361098C	7527 Rockcrest	$ 274,000	$280,000	1209	723498	06/02/2016	RIDGE

Figure 8. Unfiltered MLS Data Search

How to Make Feature Adjustments

Where there are calculable differences, adjust the features considered between each comparable sale and the subject property. Never modify the subject, only the comparables. The goal is to change the comparable home to make it like the subject, on paper. Not all features will require adjustment. Sometimes the compared feature shows the comparable is less valuable than the subject. In these circumstances, add value to that feature to bring it up to the subject property. Sometimes the feature of the comparable is more valuable than the same feature on the

FEATURE	SUBJECT	COMPARABLE SALE #1	+(−)$ Adjustment	COMPARABLE SALE #2	+(−)$ Adjustment	COMPARABLE SALE #3	+(−)$ Adjustment
Address	4550 Hillcrest Dr, Green Bay, WI 54313	1140 Pleasant Valley Dr, Oneida, WI 54155		965 Thornberry Creek Dr, Oneida, WI 54155		4427 Gypsy Ln, Oneida, WI 54155	
Proximity to Subject		0.76 miles SW		0.97 miles SW		1.41 miles W	
Sale Price	$	$ 520,000		$ 410,000		$ 490,000	
Sale Price/Gross Liv. Area	$ sq. ft.	$ 144.61 sq. ft.		$ 160.22 sq. ft.		$ 149.57 sq. ft.	
Data Source(s)		MLS #50039330;DOM93		MLS #50044703;DOM 283		MLS #50058049;DOM 51	
Verification Source(s)		RANW MLS/Assessor		RANW MLS/Assessor		RANW MLS/Assessor	
VALUE ADJUSTMENTS	DESCRIPTION	DESCRIPTION	+(−)$ Adjustment	DESCRIPTION	+(−)$ Adjustment	DESCRIPTION	+(−)$ Adjustment
Sales or Financing Concessions	ArmLth Conv. 1000	ArmLth Conv. 1000		ArmLth Conv. 0	−1,000	ArmLth Cash: 0	
Date of Sale/Time	s11/11: Unk	s11/11: Unk		s08/12: Unk		s06/12: Unk	
Location	N: Res;	N: Res;		N: Res;		N: Res;	
Leasehold/Fee Simple	Fee Simple	Fee Simple		Fee Simple		Fee Simple	
Site	12.04 ac	36113 sf	+56,100	32670 sf	+56,500	6.5 ac	+27,700
View	N: Res; Woods	N: Res; Woods		N: Res; Woods		N: Res; Woods	
Design (Style)	Colonial	Contemporary		Ranch	0	Ranch	0
Quality of Construction	Q2	Q2		Q2		Q2	
Actual Age	38	11	0	14	0	20	0
Condition	C2	C2		C2		C2	
Above Grade Room Count	Total 7 / Bdrms. 3 / Baths 2.1	Total 8 / Bdrms 3 / Baths 3.0	−2,000	Total 6 / Bdrms 3 / Baths 2.1		Total 6 / Bdrms 1 / Baths 1.0	0
Gross Living Area	2,877 sq. ft.	3,596 sq. ft.	−25,200	2,559 sq. ft.	+11,100	3,276 sq. ft.	−14,000
Basement & Finished	1679sf0sfin	2759sf800sfin	−12,000	2559sf1100sfin	−16,500	3752sf2002sfwo	−30,000
Rooms Below Grade	1rr1br1.0ba0o	1rr1br1.0ba0o	0	1rr1br1.0ba1o	0	0rr3br3.0ba1o	0
Functional Utility	Typ For Age	Typ For Age		Typ For Age		Typ For Age	
Heating/Cooling	GFA/AC	GFA/AC		GFA/AC		GFA/AC	
Energy Efficient Items	Typ For Age	Typ For Age		Typ For Age		Typ For Age	
Garage/Carport	3 Car Attached	4 Car Attached	−3,000	3 Car Attached		3 Car Attached	
Porch/Patio/Deck	Patio	Patio		Patio		None	+2,000
Fireplace	(2)FP's	(1)FP	+2,500	(2)FP's		None	+5,000
Shed/Fence/Pool	None	None		None		None	
Misc	None	None		None		None	
Net Adjustment (Total)		☒ + ☐ −	$ 15,400	☒ + ☐ −	$ 51,100	☒ + ☐ −	$ −4,300
Adjusted Sale Price of Comparables		Net Adj. 3.0% / Gross Adj. 19.6%	$ 535,400	Net Adj. 12.5% / Gross Adj. 20.5%	$ 461,100	Net Adj. 0.9% / Gross Adj. 17.1%	$ 485,700

Figure 9. The comparable adjustment table

subject. In these circumstances, subtract value from that feature to bring it down to the subject property. The formula for adjusting comparables is plus (+) if the subject is better and minus (–) if the subject is lesser. For example, Figure 9 shows the actual comparable adjustment table from an actual appraisal. You will find a similar adjustment table in all residential appraisals and in a well-done BPO.

In this comparable adjustment table (shown in Figure 9), 4550 Hillcrest Drive (subject) has a large lot (called the "site" in the feature column on the left-hand side of the form). Following that "site" row across the page, all of the comparables sites are smaller. The appraiser demonstrated that they recognize the subject is superior to all the comparables and placed a dollar value on the significance of that difference. The "+" symbol in front of the value indicates they adjusted the value to the comparable properties to make them equal to the subject. The "site" row on Figure 9 is outlined in black ink.

Also in the feature column is a line that says "gross living area." The subject is 2,877 square feet. Two comparables are larger, and one is smaller. Again the appraiser recognized the differences and accounted for them in the values of the comparables: –25,200, +11,100, and –14,000 dollars. The minuses (–) bring the value of the larger comparables down to make them equal to the subject. The one plus (+) brings the smaller property up to be equal to the subject. The "gross living area" row on Figure 9 is outlined in black ink.

Every feature the appraiser considered worthy of either an upward or downward adjustment is accounted for on the face of that page in the appraisal document. The final row is named Adjusted Sale Price of Comparables and is where the reconciliation of all the adjustments is tabulated against the actual sale price of the comparable. Comparable number three sold for $490,000 and, after adjustments to $485,700, suggests that it is now worth the same as the subject property. The "range of value" in this appraiser's opinion is between $461,100 and $535,400, a $75,300 difference between the low and high end of the range of value. The "Adjusted Sale Price of Comparables" row on Figure 9 is outlined in black ink.

How to Determine Individual Feature Adjustments

The chart in Figure 10 (on the next page) demonstrates suggested price adjustments of the key features in a typical American home. Median value is a home selling for about $230,000. If prices where you live are higher or lower, the suggested key adjustments may require modification. You and your agent can determine if these adjustments need some tweaking. A better source may be an appraiser in your area willing to share his or her thoughts on particular adjustments, or, if you have an appraisal available, you can calculate what the appraiser is thinking about the specific adjustments. For example, in the Hillcrest Drive appraisal above, the appraiser assigned a value of $3,000 for the extra stall on an attached garage.

A Few Additional Tips

If the total adjustments of a comparable sale home's amenities are more than 25 percent of the value of the subject property, you need to ask yourself whether you have the best comparables. In most cases, you should try to find others, even if the sale date is

Item	Standard adjustments	Comments
Design / Style of Home	No adjustment if same style	
Exterior Finish – Full or Partial	$5,000 to $30,000	Brick/Stone/Plastic/Aluminum
Main Level Square Footage	$10 to $50+ per square foot	Typical falls within $15 to $30
Full Bath Count	$1,000 to $8,000+	Depends on type of home
Half Bath Count	$500 to $4,000+	Depends on type of home
Master Bath		Market Driven
Bedroom Count	$500 to $5,000+	Depends on type of home
Total Room Count	No adjustment	
Garage Stalls	$500 to $5,000+ per stall	Depends on type of home
Garage Detached		Market Driven
Basement – Partial	$5 to $40+ per square foot	for sq. ft. difference built
Basement – Finished	$5 to $40+ per square foot	In addition to none/partial
As the following are more subjective	they are more difficult to adjust	examine the market closely
Location	Adjusted if market dictates	
Age	over 10–20 years are adjusted	$100–$1,000 per year
Split Bedrooms	$1,000 to $3,000	Very localized
Condition	$5,000 to $20,000+ of home	Depends on condition rating
Site (Lot Size)	No adjustment within 10%	
Landscaping	No adjustment	Market dictates over improve?
Custom Amenities	No adjustment	Included in Quality Construction
Porch, Patios, Decks	$500 to $5,000+	Add for 3 Seasons, Gazebos
Quality of Construction	$5,000 to $100,000	Depends on economy to luxury
Central Air Conditioning & Fireplace	$500 to $5,000+	Depends on type of home
Barns, Pole Buildings, Outbuildings	$1,000 to $20,000+	Depends on size and use
Sheds & Fences	$500 to $5,000+	
Swimming Pools (inground)	$2,000 to $20,000+	Climate and popularity

Figure 10. Feature Adjustment Guide

older. In this circumstance, you will calculate an adjustment for the time of the sale. If homes have increased in value by 2 percent per annum and the sale date was three years ago, you would add 6 percent of the sale price for a time-of-sale adjustment.

Most agents skip driving by the comparable properties. In some cases, they have seen them before at a showing or a listing presentation. Appraisers, however, are required to drive by the comparables, which adds considerable weight to your decision as to which comparables are good ones. In addition to the homes you may have viewed at an open house, you can learn a lot by driving by the comparables yourself, especially those in the neighborhoods in which you live or would like to live. You may spot a yard sign on a home that competes well with the property you are evaluating.

A lack of good comparables creates a wider range of value. This fact is the reason that rural property, atypical homes, or exceptionally high-valued homes are difficult to evaluate.

Consider practicing with a few homes. See how close to predicting the final sale price you can get with home sales in the neighborhood. Many classes that teach students how to buy stocks, for instance, practice in class before they invest. A home is a much larger investment, so it makes sense to practice predicting a few home sales when there is nothing at risk. Look to the great training conducted by individuals in music or sports, and mimic what they do to succeed.

Professional athletes first perform regular exercises daily; then they perform specific routines designed to improve muscle memory and strength for specific tasks they need to compete— for years. Musicians play the same chords over and over again, training their fingers and their minds to achieve an absolute pitch as long as they continue to play. Reading and studying the six chapters in this book takes almost no time by comparison but will serve you better personally than watching an athlete or musician perform, and the knowledge you gain will stay with you forever.

In summary, then, the correct path in evaluating a home is to gather information about the five considerations in determining a property's value. This information is the same information utilized by professional appraisers. The most significant of these five factors in understanding value is the comparable sales exercise demonstrated in the comparable sales table. Sifting through the data for similar homes that have sold in the neighborhood in the past six to twelve months to determine which three properties are most like the subject requires study. Calculating a value for the differences between the subject and each comparable requires research and logic. Calculating the differences between the subject property in each comparable sale requires math skill.

Your agent is the best person to gather the data to be researched because they have it at their fingertips by way of the MLS. You had also collected information on potential comparables when you attended open houses or viewed a home privately. The essential features in each home are the most vital piece of the adjustments. Selecting the three comparables closest to the subject property with all or most of these features requires thought and judgment. Applying reflection and analysis takes time. The comparables picked and the individual adjustment calculations have an enormous impact on the appraiser's opinion of value.

So while your agent is the best person to gather the raw data, the agent may not be the best person to select the last three comparables or judge which key components to adjust and what dollar amount of each adjustment is proper. This point in determining a property's value is where your newly acquired knowledge comes to the forefront. As the broker of a large real estate company for many years, I witnessed some of the highest sales producers in the organization struggle with picking the right comparables and making the logical adjustments when they came to me for guidance. These were individuals who had been practicing real estate for years.

Sharing this appraisal weakness is not information the buyer or seller will ever hear. "I want you to know I am not skilled at the appraising of property, so would you mind looking over my shoulder" is rarely, if ever, transmitted to the customer or client. I believe many agents are not aware they are not very good at it, and agents who know they are not good at evaluating property dismiss the value of the comparable sale adjustment table. Agents who produce an accurate work product understand the importance of applying proven appraisal techniques and use that knowledge to benefit their customers and clients.

Finally, determine the number of comparable neighborhood homes that are currently competing to gauge the marketplace. Then ask your agent to look back to this date last year and calculate how many homes came onto the market in the following six months. As an example, if the sales rate is three homes per month and there are only two competing homes, the seller is in the driver's seat. If there are forty comparable homes for sale, the buyer is in the driver's seat. So look at the range of value you determined and the current sales trend and project the future environment to help you make the best decision on your initial asking (or offering) price.

So many times buyers and sellers alike are negotiating hard on price, when they have no solid basis for their opinion. This is a weak position to be in when you are buying or selling your largest single asset. This single point is the main reason real estate transactions fail in negotiations. Now that you understand the only acceptable method to evaluate property, you are in a much stronger position to negotiate, so let us move on to negotiating.

Frank Asks: We listed our home with a company three weeks ago, and we have some concerns about the real estate agent's marketing of our home. I emailed him (so as to document it) and voiced my concerns about using MLS only. There are no signs for an open house, and I have to initiate the phone calls to the broker. We are in our third week and had just two prospective buyers. When we listed our home with this broker, he said he had at least four prospective buyers interested in our location. We are still waiting. What are my options if things don't change?

Dear Monty's Answer: I do not know your relationship with your agent. Have you done business with him in the past? Have you spent much time with him? What made you decide to choose the agent? Did the agent make any promises to you? Was an action plan discussed? Were multiple agents interviewed? How was the asking price determined? How long ago was the email sent? Is the agent the designated broker in the office or under the supervision of another broker? Were your expectations discussed during the listing process?

The listing agreement is a personal services contract. The contract is between you and the real estate company or broker, not the agent. Most brokers work hard to manage and coach their agents and have set protocols to respond to customers' concerns. You have not yet asked for a release; for this reason, we do not know what the broker will do. Some brokers will simply release you; some will want a fee for releasing you; others will work hard to dissuade you.

A Suggestion

Call the agent and set an appointment to meet with him face to face. Do not attempt to voice your concerns on the telephone. Meeting in his office elevates the importance of the discussion. Only make the appointment to meet with him. Try to meet at his office during regular business hours or perhaps on a Saturday morning.

Go to the meeting with a written agenda, and ask for an action plan. Share your concerns and frustration, but maintain control, as in not to shout, threaten, or be disrespectful. As the saying goes, "One gains more with an ounce of sugar than with a pound of salt." Agree on what, when, and where these action plans will take place at each point.

If you get an agreement, organize your notes about what was agreed. Send a follow-up email confirming your understanding of the conversation and ask him to respond by a certain date if his opinion is different. Hopefully, this meeting will result in a better understanding of expectations between you. It may go well from here, and your concerns may be addressed.

If the situation does not improve, your next step is to call again, but this time, request the designated broker to intervene and join the meeting. If the agent balks, call the broker yourself. Repeat the process.

Now, after this discussion, there are several choices on your course of action:

- Give the agent more time if the broker agrees.

- Ask to be reassigned to an agent the broker believes can meet your expectations.

- Ask to be released from the listing agreement through the use of a cancellation and mutual release form that frees you to list with another broker with no cost or obligation.

It seems logical that the broker might agree to release you if you handle the situation in this fashion. Having given them the opportunity to perform, they have failed to do so under the broker's supervision, and now your only satisfactory alternative is to ask to terminate the agreement.

Food for Thought

It appears you want to sell the home quickly. Is your agent aware of this fact? Are you aware of market conditions in the neighborhood? Two showings in the first three weeks may be spectacular. When I think of open houses, open-house signs are present. There are exceptions in certain communities with rules and restrictions that prevent yard signs. Could that be the case here?

Are your expectations too high? Did the agent set them high in his enthusiasm to convince you to choose him?

Or are high hopes simply a part of your personality? As you suggested, you may be stuck with this contract until it expires. Keeping the discussion on a business level increases your odds of terminating the relationship in the best possible way.

ASK MONTY

James Asks: On impulse, I gave an agent friend a one-year contract to sell my home. I went with her because she stressed her experience of thirty years, but after four or five months, there is no result. Not even a showing. Can I back out of our deal by telling her we are not selling anymore?

Dear Monty's Answer: Every state handles terminating listings a bit differently. Your email did not include a lot of information necessary to give you accurate advice. Some examples of helpful hints would be these: Is your friend updating you regularly? What does she say as to why no showings? Who established the price? Why were you selling it five months ago? Has your motive changed, or are you planning on relisting with another company?

Without much data to go on, here is what I might do if it was my friend. I would have a heart-to-heart talk with her. Tell her you are unhappy (she may be unhappy, or embarrassed, as well).

If I were planning on relisting with someone else, I would not tell her I was taking it off the market. If another company is in your plans, you should tell her and ask for a cancellation and mutual release document that frees you to list with someone else. If you told her you did not want to sell, and she agreed and only stopped marketing and showing it, but then you listed with someone else, you may ultimately have liability for two commissions.

If you are taking the home off the market because you changed your mind, I would still ask for a release agreement. The reason for a release is different here. If someone came to her and wanted to pay full price for the house during the remaining listing term, and she came with that offer, and you rejected it, you may be liable for the commission even if you dismissed the offer.

If you still want to sell, ask her why there have been no showings. If she set the price, ask her if she made a mistake. And if she did make a mistake, where should the price be now to create interest? Consider negotiating an agreement that she is given another thirty to sixty days at the lower price, but if nothing changes, she will release you. The best way to accomplish this is to amend the listing contract by lowering the price and changing the expiration date.

5

HOW TO NEGOTIATE

AH, THE FINE ART OF THE DEAL. But often ego, misinformation, or just downright stubbornness costs a sale unnecessarily. In most cases, one (or both) parties were not willing to consider the concern or objection of the other party.

The real estate negotiation process is where discussion and decisions about what each side wants will take place. It is often the point in the transaction where one side or both buyer and seller become silent or evasive on what they want, out of fear that communicating their needs will somehow weaken their negotiating position. The actual negotiating takes place in writing, in the form of contractual offers, counteroffers, rejections, and new offers. A contract of sale is created when the parties reach agreement in writing to the terms they have been discussing.

A book titled *Getting More,* written by Stuart Diamond, a professor at Wharton Business School, who developed and tested over forty years a new model for negotiating, demonstrates a method that is more successful, more often, than traditional theories about negotiating. Two key factors discussed in the book are about the importance of transparency and credibility in the negotiation process.

Because buyer and seller often have decidedly different needs and priorities, negotiations can become emotionally frustrating and confusing at times. Learning more about the concept of negotiation can help guide you to a fair agreement between parties.

Be Informed

Accurate information is the best tool you can have during negotiations. Understanding a home's condition, its range of value, and the many other aspects that affect value will help you negotiate with confidence. It's also important to be aware of and consider the other party's circumstances and the thinking that is driving their negotiations.

Both sides should also be aware of the actual sales and competitive property statistics in the submarket in which the home is located, which has to do with neighborhood characteristics and truly comparable homes. If one party has better information than the other, the party with less information is at risk. An example of risk for a seller is rejecting a good offer based on emotion or on their mortgage balance instead of the market. For buyers, the risk is losing a home they wanted because they tried to buy for less than the market or, worse yet, paid too much for a home. It is your responsibility to obtain this information. It is your real estate agent's job to deliver the information to you.

Seek first to understand, and then seek to be understood. To understand the negotiating process, you should first appreciate the impact of different levels of interest or motivation. Consider how differently you would approach negotiating with the other party if "you had to sell or buy" versus "you would sell or buy for the right offer" were the circumstances.

Such differences, whether large or small, can create a stressful environment for everyone involved. This point in time is when all the effort you have invested in learning, coupled with experience, will help guide you. This point in time is when your observations, collection of information, and ability to ask the right questions throughout the steps of the real estate process will come to fruition.

First, get agreement with your agent. Your agent is a highly beneficial resource here. Without an intermediary, people who are negotiating tend to take fixed positions faster and more firmly. While some agents are expert negotiators, many agents fall short in this step in the real estate process. There will be circumstances when you are interviewing agents in which you can test them. One of the questions you might ask is if they see themselves as a good negotiator. After they answer, ask them for a story where their negotiating skill saved a transaction; strong negotiators tend to remember those successes.

A more direct way to test their negotiating skill is to ask them to reduce their fee from, say, six to five percent. Do they agree without any pushback? Do they act shocked, or offended, as if they had never been asked that question? Does the question ruffle them? Do they offer a plausible explanation as to why they cannot honor your request? With this conversation fresh in your mind, think about how they may react to a question about reducing the price on a home.

Not to be confused with being credible and transparent with the facts, here is an example about why sticking to the facts is important. An agent can unwittingly pour gasoline on the fire by offering little sidebars to the other agent that are transmitted back to their customer, instead of strictly communicating the facts. You can prevent this by being careful about what personal information you share with your agent. For example, if you are leaving for Paris next Wednesday, and you are countering a buyer's offer with a $5,000 uptick, tell your agent you need an answer by Tuesday, but don't tell the agent it is because you are going to Paris. An offhand remark could affect the buyer's response: "What? They want another five grand, and they are on the way to Paris! Forget it." Your agent would have been better off demonstrating to the other agent the comparables and adjustments you used to justify the counteroffer.

It is helpful for you and your agent to agree on the most appropriate tactics to employ. For instance, if you were a buyer, would a note to the seller about why you love the house help or hurt negotiations? As a seller, would a personal note back to the prospective buyer with your counteroffer sway that buyer's thinking? Sometimes these notes help, sometimes not. Also, remember that although different styles and personalities will surface during negotiations, buyer and seller share the same mission: to achieve their goal while protecting their best interests. Remember that your agent has access to all the up-to-date market information that you need to make the right decisions.

In working with your agent, keep these considerations in mind:

▸ **Their best customers are other real estate agents.** The high rate of co-brokerage, real estate board activities, and familiarity can create relationships. These relationships can sometimes be advantageous but can also work against you. For example, as a seller, you want to counteroffer back to the buyer. Your agent knows from past experience that this action will be viewed negatively by the buyer's agent, who is obligated to deliver the counteroffer to the buyer. Will your agent share her experience and suspicion with you? Will your agent be ready to demonstrate the logic of the counteroffer? Or will your agent simply push you to accept the offer? The best course of action in this situation is to ask your agent for updated market information in your submarket and review market activity to date on your home before you decide to counter the offer. This update may also help you to determine the amount of the counteroffer.

▶ **Much of an agent's training is focused on finding new customers,** not appraisal techniques and negotiation— the value of a home is one area in which the customer is most likely to experience a degradation in service. As an example, if your agent refers to an online real estate website as the source of his value conclusion on your home, your red flag should be waving. It should be waving because value opinions derived from the Internet without the inclusion of a physical inspection are not dependable. Additionally, if you are not up to speed on the basics of the real estate appraisal process, you often will not even realize an error has occurred. If your agent is not skilled enough in appraisals or negotiation, you may end up paying more, or selling for less, on property than you might have otherwise.

▶ **Real estate agents often have a nearly impossible job.** Keeping the details of as many as fifteen to twenty-five open client files in order at any given time and completing

the follow-up required with a variety of associated service providers, such as title companies, loan officers, and
inspection companies, can be a daunting responsibility.
Plus, they must constantly be looking for new leads and
customers outside of their current workload.

- **Fear of loss**. If your best efforts turn out to be in vain, there
will be another home (or buyer) that comes along. "Fear
of loss" is one of the primary reasons a buyer chooses a
home or a seller accepts an offer. Fear of loss is minimized
as a consideration in making negotiation decisions when
they are based on your confidence in the home's range of
value and the facts that are driving the market.

While many service businesses divide tasks by aptitude, the
real estate agent—who most likely is an independent contrac-
tor—is expected to do it all. Most people have a variety of tasks
they enjoy, and other tasks, not so much. A consequence in real
estate is that the steps in the process require very different skill
sets and attributes. My observations suggest that when an agent
is working in a step in the process that does not fit their skill sets,
their client is at risk. For example, negotiations require honesty,
patience, attention to detail, and strong communication skills. If
your agent does not exhibit these traits at this time, you should
be on high alert and call your own negotiation skills into action.

These considerations demonstrate the importance of taking the
time to educate yourself about the twelve steps in the real estate
process described on DearMonty.com so that you can anticipate
the potential issues encountered in each step beforehand.

Point-Counterpoint

Let's take a look at the different points of view that buyer and seller have during a negotiation.

The buyer wants to know

- Why are they selling?
- How was the price determined?
- Have they had other offers?
- How long has the home been on the market?
- Will they come down on the price?
- Should I act firm or noncommittal about my offer?
- How can I avoid overpaying without starting so low that the seller does not take me seriously?
- Will my financing contingency (an FHA loan, or 100 percent financing) or occupancy needs (we can't move in until our lease expires) affect my ability to negotiate?
- When should I introduce other aspects, such as poor condition or slow market, that affect the price?

The seller wants to know

- How serious is this buyer?
- How was their offering price determined?
- Have they made offers on other homes?
- How long have they been looking?
- Will they go higher on their offer?

- How long should I wait to lower my asking price, if at all?

- If I get a full-price offer within the first week or two, are we underselling our home?

- Can the buyer acquire financing?

- Do they have enough earnest money?

- How important is the time of occupancy to me? Some buyers want to move in before closing (not a good idea, in most cases), and some sellers want six months to move out. Again, there are many reasons occupancy can be a deal breaker or test your negotiating skills to the limit.

As you can see, both buyer and seller have concerns over the same subjects. Your best negotiating results will occur if you studied and implemented the strategies described in this guide and you have chosen a competent agent to help guide you through this stage in the process. Your agent is communicating with the other person's agent. It is his or her job to provide you with accurate, timely, and unbiased analysis of the pros and cons of every decision for you to consider, to find the answers to all of your questions, and to help you understand the other person's position. It is your job to take the time to evaluate this information and make the decisions yourself.

By reviewing the questions buyers and sellers ask and relating them to your particular situation, you will find that the knowledge gained from these answers can help you create a smoother negotiation process and contribute to the success of the negotiation.

Let's Settle This

Dear Monty's advice to you about negotiating is to be informed. If you understand the other party's position, have a good sense of the property's range of value, and know the market dynamics in the neighborhood, you will significantly improve your chance of succeeding. Keep in mind that it takes an agreement to complete the home-buying or home-selling process. Chester Karrass, who created one of the most successful negotiation seminars in the United States, once said (and it's the title of his book), "In business as in life, you don't get what you deserve, you get what you negotiate."

You have been down most of the road. You have a better sense of the workings of the real estate industry. You know the importance of picking the best agent and how to accomplish it. You know what questions to ask about the market you are buying or selling in and can evaluate a home better than most real estate agents. And now you know how to position yourself in a negotiation. None of this will do you much good unless you read and understand the contracts! Let's move to the last piece of the puzzle.

6

UNDERSTANDING REAL ESTATE CONTRACTS

THE TWO CENTRAL CONTRACTS in residential real estate are the listing contract, between a seller and a real estate broker, and the offer to purchase, between buyer and seller. Reading and understanding these documents—*before* you sign them—and learning their implications, benefits, and consequences can make an enormous difference in the results. For example, many people do not realize the listing contract is between themselves and the agent's broker, not the agent.

Many additional forms are designed for certain events or elements that can occur within a transaction, usually available in individual states that preauthorize fill-in-the-blank real estate documents. Unlike other consumer purchases, once a real estate contract has been agreed upon and delivered, you cannot cancel it unilaterally. The only exception I am aware of is the state of New Jersey, which dictates a three-day right of rescission clause in the offer-to-purchase contract.

The Listing Contract

The listing contract is a personal services contract that lays out a road map of the broker and seller obligations and responsibilities when a broker is hired to sell a home. The real estate agent you meet with is the broker's representative, and you may never see the broker. The broker is responsible for the acts of their agents. You will be making decisions in the listing agreement that will affect many future events. Be certain you understand them.

Typical listing clauses: Forms in many states today have become quite sophisticated. Every line item in every form has potential implications. To help you prepare for listing your home, here are the most common provisions in listing agreements throughout the country:

- Identification of the participants in the contract (legal names of the seller(s) and the broker)

- Identification of the property that is for sale (a street address, a legal description, a plat map that demonstrates the size and location of the property)

- Listed price: Must be stated in the listing contract (the amount for which the seller is offering the property for sale)

- The term of contract: Start and end dates of enforceability (the date of beginning and the date of expiration of the agreement)

- Protected buyers (seller obligated for the broker commission for a stated time period when a prospect who viewed the home during the term of the contract purchases it after contract expiration)

- Seller warranty (states that there are no defects or discloses known defects)

- Broker's obligations (the work, tools, and efforts the company agrees to put forth to produce a buyer)

- Broker cooperation (the broker agrees to offer compensation to outside agents)

- Fixtures and personal property (included and excluded items on the property)

- The legal compliance disclosures (agency, lead-based paint, fair housing, and others)

- Broker compensation (the amount and conditions under which fees are due)

- Terms of sale (occupancy, earnest money, post-closing rent and more)

- Document delivery (methods and compliance timelines)

- Agency choices (seller informs broker of their agency preferences)

- Earnest money (how to manage deposits, who receives forfeited funds)

- Seller cooperation (disclosures, buyer leads, "as is" sales and more)

- Deadlines and rescission rights (implications of timing issues)

- Disclosure of material adverse facts (defects or conditions that negatively impact value that cannot be observed by the buyer)

- Right to cure (choices, and who controls them, on inspection results)

- Termination of listing (understanding parties' timing, rights, and obligations)

State-by-state philosophies and protocols are not consistent. The state law in the location of your property applies. There are instructions for gathering more information online at the end of this book to guide you.

Avoid Pocket Listings

The seller lists with one company through the "listing agent." The listing contract spells out the broker's agreement to cooperate with other brokers and their agents to gain more exposure for the home. When a sale results from the efforts of one of the cooperating companies, this is called a co-broke or co-op sale. The listing company in most markets finds the buyer less than 50 percent of the time. Larger cities typically produce higher percentages of co-op sales. Co-op sales and cooperation between brokers and real estate agents are an important part of the selling process.

A new listing is supposed to enter the MLS systems quickly, but some agents may suggest holding off until they can get their hot prospect through the house. There are several methods in which this delay can be accomplished. In some cases, the seller will agree to give the listing agent a chance to produce a buyer; in other cases, delays are created that provide an extra day or two. In other words, they want to put your home listing "in their pocket" to prevent other agents from learning about the property until their client(s) sees the house.

There is a recent trend with new listings appearing around the U.S. The words "coming soon" or similar words, may be responding to robust activity or for other reasons. If the tactics employed delay prompt MLS exposure, be careful.

Agents who promote or seek pocket listings have a conflict of interest—their earnings rise considerably with a "pocket" listing, but your property's market exposure decreases. The way you prevent this is to make certain the listing agreement is dated, and ask your agent to send you a link to the MLS listing the moment it hits the market. If an agent succeeds with a pocket listing, a question you will never know the answer to is this: Were other buyers in the marketplace willing to pay more?

Examine the Contract Before Signing

When you are planning to list your home, first request a blank copy of the listing contract, and read it before you interview agents. This gives you time to focus on the wording of the contract itself, letting you then concentrate on the agents themselves in the listing presentations. During a listing presentation, an agent will use comparable home sales to explain market conditions in your neighborhood, talk about the best tactics to maximize your home's value, and explain why he or she is the best agent for you.

As you read through the blank contract, write down any questions you have, and ask about these issues during your agent interviews. Pay attention to each agent's reaction and responses; they will give you insight into their view of the importance of reviewing documents. Their willingness to set aside time to explain the listing package and answer your questions speaks volumes and may be a critical indicator of the service level you can expect.

Listing Myths

Real estate myths have circulated for generations; the industry may actually have more armchair quarterbacks than football. Here are a few common misperceptions:

- **The listing agent will be the person who finds the buyer.** The reason this is a myth is simply the numbers. If there were a hundred buyers searching the market for a home like yours, many listing agents might have one or two candidates for the house. Therefore, the chances of another agent completing a transaction are very high. Many agents leave the impression they will be the one to find the buyer, and they want to find the buyer, but the odds are stacked against them.

- **There is no three-day right of rescission, as with other consumer contracts.** The only exception is the state of New Jersey. A listing contract is a personal services contract, and early termination is negotiated between the parties to the contract.

- **Open houses are a waste of everyone's time.** In reality, open houses work. While it is true that not everyone who walks through the door is a buyer for your home, buyers walk through that door with regularity. While there are homes that are exceptions, such as those that are over-priced, in remote areas, or in poor condition, agents who believe open houses are a waste of time have a hidden agenda; they must pay for ads; they like weekends with family; or they have too many listings to service.

- **The home will sell very quickly.** Some homeowners are disappointed and take it personally when a prospect decides not to buy their home, or they want to believe many buyers will want it. In certain markets a home may sell quickly, but in most markets it may take time and a number of viewers before the buyer appears. Sometimes an early looker will come back to the house a month or two later. There is also a correlation between price and time on market. Assuming the range of value on your home is accurate, if you price your home at or under the bottom of your home's range of value, it will sell quickly.

- **The home has a particular value.** No home has a value; every home has a range of value. That range of value widens as the number of recent comparable sales diminishes.

- **Experienced agents are the best agents.** I started selling real estate when I was twenty-one. I had no prior experience. In my first twelve months, I completed sixty-four transactions with no assistants. There were zero consumer complaints. I credit an excellent broker who trained me well and spent time with me. The feedback from buyers and sellers was that I worked hard, understood their needs, worked efficiently, and was honest and humble (my broker kept reminding me to stay humble). I told everyone I worked with I would treat them like my mother and father, and I did.

While longevity can be a valuable asset, it is by no means an indication the person has the important skills necessary to deliver the service necessary to maximize the consumer experience. Dear Monty has chosen many real estate agents with only a year or two of experience. There are many real estate professionals in the business for a short period of time I would choose over someone with "twenty-five years' experience." This is a myth started and perpetuated by "experienced" agents.

The two most important issues in placing your home on the market are agent selection and proper pricing. Including the listing agreement and its implications for discussion with prospective agents will provide you with more information and feedback that will help you make the best choice in agents. The pricing strategy will depend on your circumstances. In some cases, if you have no deadlines, and the market conditions are right, testing the market at the top end of the range of value can make sense. If you have a deadline, perhaps being the next home to sell makes the most sense. Together you can set the best price for your property.

The Most Influential Document: The Offer to Purchase

Without question, the offer to purchase is the most powerful document you will be asked to sign in a real estate transaction. In many respects, the physical closing at the title company, weeks or months in the future, is simply a confirmation of what happened the day the offer became a contract. This point in time can be stressful and scary, or it can be exciting and satisfying. The difference is based on what you know about how you got here and how you made your choices—choices based on facts, experience, and emotional restraint.

If your best efforts turn out to be in vain, there will be another home (or buyer) that comes along. "Fear of loss" is one of the primary reasons a buyer chooses a home or a seller accepts an offer. Fear of loss gains, or loses, importance as a consideration based on your real estate knowledge and local submarket facts.

Never Sign a Real Estate Contract without Reading and Understanding It

To become familiar and comfortable with the offer to purchase before you get involved with the details of actually signing an offer is the best example. Do not wait until your agent is asking you to sign this document to read it for the first time. Ask one of the agents you interview to provide a blank copy of the offer-to-purchase form so you can be well prepared when it is time to negotiate. Asking for this document tests the agent's follow-up, and you can use the document early. Reserve some time to become familiar with it. Have a notepad at your side in which to write questions. Read the fine print!

It is a good practice to read a completed copy in advance of signing every document in a real estate transaction. Technology has made it easy to share documents electronically. While completing all the documents at the kitchen table or on the hood of a car can be convenient, there is no reason for not reading documents in advance. We are all accustomed to agreeing to terms of use without reading them when we sign into websites, but it is much more personal and perilous when buying and selling real estate.

Let Us Promote an Understanding

Many states print approved real estate forms. When states forgo designing real estate forms, it is typical for the local or regional MLS or National Association of Realtors local organization to step forward with the necessary forms.

Remember that your offer becomes a contract of sale when accepted and delivered as written. You do not want to leave any question unanswered unless you have protection with a well-written contingency. A contingency in an offer to purchase revolves around a question that takes time and expense to answer correctly after the offer is accepted. For example, if you need a mortgage, you make the offer contingent upon obtaining it. The contingency must contain all the details—the amount of the mortgage, the amount of time it will take to receive a commitment, the specific terms, the payment amount, and more. Other common contingencies are for inspections and the closing of another property, for example. Understanding the language and reviewing the offer beforehand should help reduce last-minute concerns and surprises.

Here are the issues most crucial to understand:

- Identity of the buyer(s) (your legal names that will be taking title)

- Description of the conveyed property (information that clearly identifies the property)

- Agency disclosure—confirms any agent representation (who your agent is representing)

- The price being proposed to pay (the agreed-upon purchase price of the property)

- Amount of earnest money and what happens to it after receipt by broker (applied to purchase price or forfeited if buyer walks away)

- Important dates and whether time is of the essence (the time frame events are to take place)

- Descriptions of issues the agreement is dependent upon (contingencies and conditions to close)

- What personal property or fixtures are included, or not, in the sale (do the draperies stay, or not)

- How to transfer the property title (type of deed provided—warranty, quit claim, executor's deed)

- Deadlines for acceptance or countering the offer (the amount of time the other party has to respond)

- Date of legal transfer—the closing date (seller receives the proceeds, and the buyer gets the deed)

- Occupancy—when the seller moves out, and when the buyer moves in (negotiated at this time)

- Penalty if occupancy requirements are not met (the penalties if buyers or sellers default)

- Representations of the owner of known defects (seller condition report)

- How financial obligations of ownership are prorated (real estate taxes, utility bills, insurance)

- Who pays for special assessments and new assessments after contract of sale is in place; how seller clears title, proves evidence of ownership, and who pays for it (most often local protocol prevails)

- What happens to the earnest money if either party fails to close? (agreement now minimizes disputes later)

- If the seller reneges on the sale, can the buyer force the seller to close anyway? Likewise, if the buyer fails to close, can the seller sue for damages? (laws vary by state; understanding these laws when you sign this document can minimize surprises later)

- What if there is a fire? (explains at what point each party can walk and when they cannot)

- Acknowledgment that the contract is a legal document (both parties declare they understand it)

- Signature area for buyer(s) (a place on the documents for the buyer to sign)

- Reinforcement of the binding nature of the agreement (there are consequences here, so be sure you understand)

- Signature area for the seller to accept, reject, or counter the offer (a place on the document for the seller to sign)

Counteroffers, Addendums, Notices, and Amendments

It is common to include addendums and contingencies with any offer. Subjects such as financing, the sale of other property, acceptance of transfer, receiving an inheritance, or many other circumstances become part of offers to purchase. These additional forms provide time to obtain reports that are not practical to invest in without a definitive agreement.

When a seller rejects an offer, either by written notice or by responding with a counteroffer, the communication must be in writing. A nonresponse, which means silence until the time limit for acceptance has expired, is also a rejection. It is hazardous to take the shortcut of verbal communication for a variety of reasons. The main reason is that oral contracts are not enforceable in real estate.

It is important to understand how to maintain provisions from the original offer with a counter offer. You will want to be able to see in the document or documents the words that confirm your expectations. It is not uncommon in the heat of the back-and-forth negotiations between buyer and seller for some relevant provision to slip through the cracks.

Here's an example. Let's say the original offer listed a number of personal items the buyer wanted. In the ensuing counteroffers back and forth, the seller countered but left the upright freezer out of the second counteroffer, and no one noticed. The nuances of real estate contract law vary somewhat from state to state, which is another good reason to become familiar with the forms in the state in which you will be conducting business. Does the buyer still get the freezer? Maybe not.

ASK MONTY

Beth Asks: When selling an existing home and buying a new one, should we list our current home with a contingency that they have to wait for us to find a new home before we will close? Or should we find a new home and make an offer with the contingency we have to sell our current home first?

Dear Monty Advises: Hello, Beth, and thank you for your question. I do not know enough about a variety of circumstances that apply to your situation, but I can offer up information that may help you make the best decision on how to proceed.

What Comes First?

Evaluating the risk of owning two homes—should you buy or sell first—is a common dilemma that homeowners face today. In fact, about 70 percent of home buyers are also home sellers. People caught in this time trap are often faced with difficult questions and weighty decisions to make. The first and most critical assessment you must make is to understand your needs, priorities, and finances. You are then ready to evaluate your options, choose one that suits your needs, and then develop a plan to follow.

The Evaluation Process

The following chart will assist you in evaluating your time trap. The approaches are listed vertically on the left-hand side of the chart. Important aspects to consider are listed horizontally along the top of the chart. The *yes, no,* and *possibly* appearing in the body of the chart indicate the impact each option may have on the various considerations. For example, if you decide to sell and rent temporary living space, will you be able to avoid double moves with the movers? The answer is no.

You will need to determine how valuable each consideration is and base your decision on which approach best meets your needs. I encourage you to discuss your options with family, your lender, and your real estate agent before proceeding.

Caution: There will be exceptions to these general statements in the Time Trap Evaluation Tool.

The "Time Trap" Evaluation Tool

if I decide to	will I be able to...								general comments
	hold out for the top price on my old home?	avoid limiting the number of buyers on the old home?	avoid the risk of owning two homes?	avoid double moves with the movers?	avoid limiting my choices and time to look?	avoid being bumped by another buyer?	negotiate for the best price and terms on the new home?	buy new home knowing what my proceeds will be?	
sell my home, contingent on finding a new home	possibly	no	yes	possibly	no	yes	yes	yes	most buyers will not want to wait for you to find a new home
buy a new home contingent on selling the old home	no	yes	yes	possibly	yes	no	no	no	you may not have adequate time to effectively sell your old home
sell and rent a temporary living space	yes	yes	yes	no	yes	yes	yes	yes	will have a double move and the process may take longer
sell with a long occupancy clause	no	no	yes	possibly	no	yes	possibly	yes	most buyers want to move in soon
enter into a guarantee sale agreement	no	yes	yes	yes	yes	yes	yes	yes	you may receive a lower price than if you had time to wait for the eventual buyer
buy and hope my home sells	no	yes	no	yes	yes	yes	yes	no	making dual mortgage payments can be a burden

Image: ericamontgomery.com

Figure 11. The Time Trap Evaluation Tool

Now, Make Your Plan of Attack

When you develop your plan, consider these factors:

- Demand and marketability of your old home

- Cost of owning an extra home

- Impact of the eventual selling price of your old home and the time it will take to sell and close

- Cost of having to move twice

- Your intensity and motivation to make the change

To determine which plan best fits your situation, carefully weigh the strategic effects of all the options. Your decision should revolve around the concepts of risk management, financial ability, and personal motivation.

A True Story

A husband and wife are going to open houses as they are casually looking to downsize from their large, stately, turn-of-the-century home to a smaller, newer property. They made many enjoyable improvements over the years to their home, but the work became overwhelming. They came across the perfect house, and they loved it. Because this home was new on the market, the agent explained there was a lot of interest in it. Trying to contain their excitement, they asked the agent (a longtime friend and experienced agent) to take a look at their old home and tell them what it was worth. The agent proceeded to do a broker price opinion (BPO) and came back to them with his analysis: "It's worth about $225,000, and I can sell it within sixty days."

The couple decided that they should go ahead and buy the new home. They said, "We'll worry about the old house later," and made the purchase without a home sale contingency. They moved into the new home, put their old home up for sale, and lived happily ever.

Wait! It did not end quite that well. As you may have guessed, the old house did not sell for what the agent thought, and it did not sell within sixty days. Almost two years of mortgage and upkeep payments later, they accepted an offer far below what they expected.

As you read this account, you can clearly see what they failed to do to protect themselves at the time. In part, you can see it because you have the benefit of looking at this situation from an objective point of view. Would they have done the same thing if they had it to do all again? It is easy to second-guess the situation. Each year, similar scenarios play out this way many times throughout the United States.

It Pays to Plan

This time trap issue can be an extremely difficult one. Because each of the various solutions for this dilemma involves expense, it is vital that you carefully assess your needs and options before you proceed. By conscientiously planning your approach and understanding the risks and costs involved, you should be able to avoid the unexpected and unwanted results that come from unplanned actions.

Can You Change the Agreement?

Contingencies are satisfied in writing with new documents as you move through the process. These new documents, called amendments or notices, are presented as the parties communicate the satisfaction or request changes to the contract contingencies. The amendment can modify the terms of the original agreement when both sides agree. These contingencies will have expiration dates—that can mean either the contract terminates or is satisfied if not removed in writing by the expiration date of the contingency. While taking the steps necessary to be able to remove the contingency is often your responsibility, your agent should also track these dates and assist you to expedite satisfying the requirements. Get out your calendar, and write in the contingency expiration dates; then ask your agent to verify them.

For example, as a buyer, your move-in date could be sooner than originally stated, but you need to make certain the seller can be out earlier. If you get agreement from the seller for that to happen, it must be in writing. Ask your agent for copies of the various forms particular to your circumstances before making or receiving an offer. You will be much more confident at this point if you review the documents and understand all the provisions beforehand.

Communicating with Email or Text Messages

Ask your questions to your agent (whether buying or selling) using email or texting. There are some reasons to use email for this task:

▶ You and the agent can exchange messages when it is convenient for each of you.

- When your questions require complicated answers, you have time to learn and consider implications before you sign anything.

- Writing questions down and answering them in writing commits each party to communicating clearly.

- Writing is more memorable than conversation.

- You have a record of the questions and answers for future reference.

If you send a text or email, and your agent responds with a telephone call to address your communication, consider following the call up with a confirmation text or email.

An old Chinese proverb will help you apply this practice and make it an active part of your process: "The strongest memory is no match for the weakest ink."

You're Almost Home

Stories of how a family member, coworker or neighbor lost his or her earnest money, had to replace a roof, or even lost their dream house are ubiquitous. Unfortunately, these occurrences often take place because consumers did not read or understand the contract and believed they could surmount issues when they appear. Buyers and sellers may not realize that problems may not appear at all (as some are invisible)—or only surface long after the transaction closes.

Hal and Rosemary Ask: When we first met our Realtor, we told her consistently that we were looking for a house that had a swimming pool or a house where the backyard was big enough to put in a swimming pool. So almost a year after we bought a house that had a backyard big enough to accommodate a swimming pool, we find out from the pool company that we got an estimate from that there's an easement in the backyard that prevents us from getting our dream pool. I talked to the Realtor and told her this new information, and she said that she wasn't aware of the easement, and she was going to pull our paperwork. She found out that there was in fact an easement. Shouldn't that have been her responsibility to have known all this before we bought the house? She's saying it was in the paperwork that we signed. Being the first house that we bought, every conversation we had with her where she used real estate jargon, we questioned her about and relied on her knowledge to guide us through the ins and outs of buying our dream house. How can this information just now come to light? Please advise.

Dear Monty's Answer: Here is how to investigate the situation to gather some facts before making a decision on what to do next. Take the following actions:

1. Go to your file from the home closing and look for the title policy or the title commitment. If there is an easement, it will be mentioned in the title report. If

you do not have that document, call the title company and ask them to email you a copy of the title documents. Also ask the title company to send you a copy of the recorded easement so you can read what it says and determine the identity of the party retaining the easement.

2. Call the pool company back and ask them to send you a copy of the document that has caused them to believe the pool cannot be constructed. If the pool company found the easement, it is possible the municipality or a utility company could hold the easement. Are there overhead utility wires along the rear lot line? Is there a backyard storm sewer? Or some other underground piping of water, natural gas, or electricity? These utilities are normally identified in some way to alert property owners of their presence. If it is a utility company, or the city, alert them to the situation, and see if they can help.

3. Look in your file for a document called a seller condition report or some similar title. In reviewing that report, look for a question where the seller is asked if there are any easements on the property. If there is a question like this on the seller condition report and the seller answered there is not an easement, it is good information to have as you sort through the situation. It could mean the easement is an error, that the seller forgot about it, or that the seller withheld the information.

4. Review the purchase agreement. Is there a contingency in the purchase agreement stating the offer is subject to the buyer determining there is no restriction on constructing a swimming pool? If that contingency is in the agreement, how was it satisfied? If it is not there, do you have any emails or text messages or notes in the file or in your computer where a written document can demonstrate the agent knew the swimming pool was important to you?

At this point, you know more about the circumstances than you did after the pool company called you. There are several possibilities:

- There is a recorded easement that was put in place for future construction that never took place and now could be abandoned. Good news for you.

- There is a recorded easement, but it is an error and was recorded against the wrong property. Again, good news for you.

- There is an active reason the easement was put in place, but the holder of the easement may have a solution that would allow them to release the easement. Cross your fingers.

- There is an active reason the easement was put in place, and it would not be possible to have it set aside. Not good news for a pool.

If this process has not uncovered a solution, and the easement is real and not to be expunged, you now have a good handle on the situation. This is helpful in presenting the facts to an attorney licensed in the state in which the property is located to get a legal opinion as to your options.

You did not mention whether the pool you are planning is an in-ground or above-ground pool. While it remains unclear about the elements of the easement and its purpose, if you are thinking about an above-ground pool, you may have some negotiation power with the easement holder.

Once you have an opinion and some guidance as to how to proceed, you can decide on your next steps.

Problems also happen when something as simple as an agent—or another service provider to the transaction—does not explain a sentence or paragraph correctly, or the customer misinterprets the explanation. It could also be a home seller who conceals a defect or, in the case of the elderly, forgets to disclose it. Another example is a home inspector failing to spot a major flaw. Many events can create problems in real estate transactions. While the focus of these six principles is about anticipating and preventing problems, many buyers and sellers navigate all the steps without incident.

My experiences operating real estate offices, a relocation company, consulting assignments with a national real estate franchisor, and more suggest that consumers lose more than a billion dollars every year in failed or flawed real estate transactions. We base this statement on my own organization's *known* financial disputes between buyer and seller for one year. The word *known* is inserted in the last sentence, as many times a real estate company is not involved with litigation between buyer and seller, and many buyers or sellers just absorb or settle a loss without outside intervention. We then divided the contested dollar amounts by our agent population to arrive at an average loss per agent. We obtained the billion-dollar projection by multiplying our company average per agent reported loss by the number of practicing US agents.

To my knowledge, no organization in the United States has the capability to keep track of these unexpected and unnecessary expenses. The billion-dollar guesstimate does not include the cost of lawsuits and accompanying damages that also are accrued. Because the industry is highly fragmented, and real estate company owners (and the consumers involved) tend not to share this type of information with the NAR or their competitors, it was the most logical method considered to estimate the enormity of the losses.

What does this mean for you? For an individual consumer, a $20,000 loss is enormous. In a broad sense, compare this problem to the American automobile industry taking fifty years to realize foreign companies were producing better vehicles. It took the automobile consumer buying those foreign cars in large numbers to influence the auto industry.

I believe that much in the same way as the automobile industry changed, only the consumer can lead the change in real estate. They lead it by gathering knowledge, by being alert, and taking a more active part in shaping the outcomes. When real estate agents realize that consumers of real estate services are watching closely and have a better perspective than they do, the agents will improve out of necessity.

Dear Monty's Advice

What this guide has attempted to do, without scaring you, is to reassure you that while Dear Monty is laying a bit of work and responsibility on you, digging into understanding real estate to this extent will be well worth the effort. Sad to say, studying and learning this information will make you better informed than many real estate agents and will also position you to determine which candidates make for a good agent. I firmly believe knowing how to use this information may save you thousands or tens of thousands of dollars, depending on your price point.

Human nature is not always kind. We do not always see ourselves as others see us. We often seek the path of least resistance, and, when dealing with real estate, we can sometimes temporarily become intellectually challenged or short on common sense. Or we can be smart, well educated, and see asking for help as a sign of weakness. There is an old saying in the real estate industry, "People are not in their right minds when buying and selling real estate."

Remember the story recited in chapter 4 about evaluating homes from the seller who thanked me for saving their family $50,000? While I am aware of no method to count the frequency of such occurrences, I believe the operating conditions in the day-to day real estate practices revealed in this book suggest it happens in every state, every day. The dollar amounts vary widely, the causes of the losses vary, and buyers are victims as well as the seller almost was a victim in the story above. I cannot emphasize too strongly that the only way to protect your interests is to invest the time in learning how real estate works. It will pay big dividends for you.

The goal of this book is to enlighten you. Buying and selling a home is the most complex financial transaction you will experience. The service delivery system is flawed, but it presents itself as simple. No matter your lot in life, learning to anticipate what can happen *before* it happens can save you a lot of time, frustration, and your hard-earned dollars.

I hope the time you invest in learning this process improves your real estate outcomes now and in the future.

RESOURCES

EXPLORE THESE LINKS to find unbiased, helpful information. The web links are current as of the publication of this book, but you may experience broken or bad links. Check this book's website (www.DearMonty.com) for the most current links and listings.

DEAR MONTY,

https://DearMonty.com/ My own nationally syndicated newspaper column Q&As and a description for navigating the twelve steps that consumers of real estate services encounter and property owners can use to improve their real estate outcomes. Additionally, your most pressing questions are answered, and if your circumstances are such that you need help picking a real estate agent when you are buying or selling a home, Dear Monty's Pick My Agent™ service does the heavy lifting for you. Some of the reasons buyers and sellers use the Pick My Agent™ service are, inheriting a home in a remote city, no time to invest in the necessary vetting steps, or to save money by receiving referral credits in their transaction.

Real Estate Inspection Flowchart, *www.wra.org/InspectionFlowchart,* courtesy of the Wisconsin Real Estate Magazine online edition.

American Society of Home Inspectors, *https://www.homeinspector .org/* One of several organizations that a home inspector may join to gain certification, education, and more. Use this site to find a home inspector.

Association of Real Estate License Law Officials (ARELLO), *https://www.arello.com/?SHOWNAV=1* This organization licenses, regulates, and enforces the law in the real estate industry by state. Check here to see if a prospective agent is licensed.

Case-Shiller Home Price Indices, *http://us.spindices.com/index-family/real-estate/sp-corelogic-case-shiller* Tracks home prices and changes in home prices nationally and in twenty major metropolitan areas.

Environmental Protection Agency, *https://www3.epa.gov/aircompare/* At this website you can find out if a home or property has been designated a Superfund site, meaning it is contaminated with harmful chemicals, may have been a chemical dump, or water is affected by a dump upstream. Avoid buying anything close to a Superfund site. Also a source for asbestos information can be found at *https://www.epa.gov/asbestos/protect-your-family.*

Fact Check.org, *http://www.factcheck.org/about/our-mission/* Politicians, bureaucrats, and government agencies often talk real estate–related subjects to the press. This unbiased fact checker finds truth.

Fax Zero, *http://faxzero.com/* Many companies and individuals still rely on fax machines. This service allows you to send or receive faxes online, often at no cost.

John T. Reed, *http://johntreed.com/blogs/john-t-reed-s-real-estate-investment-blog/61653315* A real estate investor and writer who offers critique of the gaggle of better-known "how to get rich quick" authors and purveyors of real estate investment advice for a fee.

Online Conversion, *http://www.onlineconversion.com/*converts many units of measurement into other units of measurement. Real estate is described in acres, sections, square feet, linear feet, and other measurements. You can validate units that are new to you here.

Pew Research Center, *http://www.pewresearch.org/* generates facts that support sound decision-making. Unbiased information on a global or national scale can be helpful to understand larger real estate issues.

Speakeasy, *https://www.speakeasy.net/speedtest/* Many of us need speed in our online habits and pay a great deal for the convenience. Use this site to test your Internet speed and relay sluggish connections to the service provider.

US **Census Bureau,** *http://www.census.gov/* You can learn about communities across the United States based on census data.

US **Debt Clock,** *http://www.usdebtclock.org/* For a reality check on how our country is doing as a whole, view the debt clock in real time. The value of our real estate depends on our country doing well.

US **Postal Service,** *https://tools.usps.com/go/ZipLookupAction!input.action* Verify a property's zip code. It is easy to get zip codes mixed up. There is much demographic information available by zip code that could affect a real estate decision.

To find helpful GIS (geographic information system, geomapping) information about a home or property, try this:

Use your browser search engine. Brown County, Wisconsin, is used as an example:

1. Type <your county, state, GIS> into your search bar, and multiple results appear. See image 1.

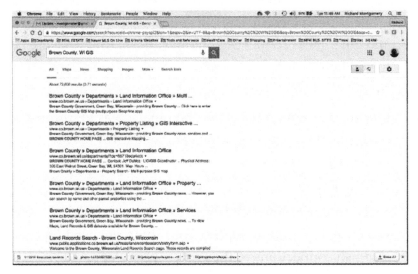

Image 1. General search

2. Click on an address that ends in .gov or .us and GIS and the log-in appears. See image 2.

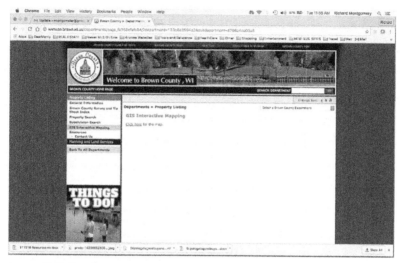

Image 2. Refined to your county search

3. Log-in page says "click here for the map," and the map and disclaimer appear. See image 3.

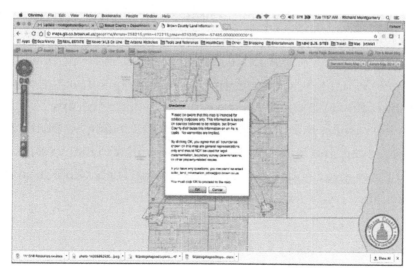

Image 3. Map is shown

4. Click on disclaimer, and the map appears ready to use. See image 4.

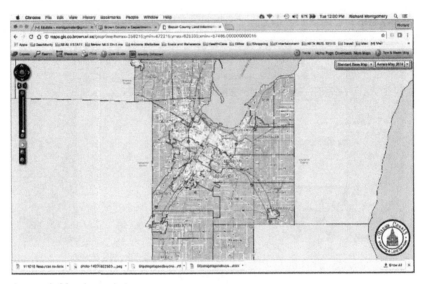

Image 4. Map is ready to use

Notice the navigation bar just above the map. There are a variety of commands you can utilize with a click. "Layers" are far left, and "Tips and news blog" are on the far right.

It will take a bit of time reading directions and experimenting to get the hang of it, but information about contour maps, aerial photos, flood plains, and more is now at your fingertips.

Remember that there are many vendors selling GIS platforms throughout the United States. They are similar in many respects, but the instruction and navigation can vary. There will be a small learning curve.

To find authoritative information about home mortgages in the United States:

Department of Housing and Urban Development (HUD), *https://www.fha.com/* Whether you need a home mortgage or a large apartment building mortgage, HUD has a variety of types of mortgage loans.

Fannie Mae, *https://www.fanniemae.com/singlefamily/mortgage-products* One of the companies that purchases loans from mortgage originators such as banks, credit unions, and online lenders. You can search to see if Fannie Mae owns your mortgage.

Freddie Mac, *http://www.freddiemac.com/* Similar to Fannie Mae with many similar programs. If Fannie Mae doesn't own your mortgage, Freddie Mac likely does.

Federal Financial Institutions Examination Council, *http://www .ffiec.gov/consumercenter.htm* A source to learn if the lender you are considering is licensed in your state. This could be helpful to know if you need a resource to help you if something goes wrong. They do not oversee state institutions, so you need to know which organization issued your lender's charter.

Mortgage Bankers Association, *https://www.mba.org/* Can be quite different from banks and credit unions in that they have access as originators to many loan products offered by different lenders that may have more variety and ways to make loans other lenders have declined.

To find real estate law, ordinances, rules, and similar data in the United States:

- Type <your state, real estate law> into your search bar and click on "enter" on your keyboard.

- Multiple results appear. Click on an address that ends in <your state.gov>

- These state sites are the source of current real estate law.

ABOUT THE AUTHOR

RICHARD MONTGOMERY has experience in a wide variety of real estate–related businesses. His involvement with methods to improve the real estate consumer experience over the past thirty years—and personal commitment—provides a unique perspective for his no-nonsense real estate advice for buyers and sellers.

As Dear Monty, he has been writing a weekly newspaper column for more than four years and is published in more than 500 newspapers around the United States. He has answered more than 2,000 questions (so far) at DearMonty.com.

Montgomery credits his early success as a real estate agent to a strong mentor who taught him to treat buyers and sellers as he would treat his own parents. He rose in the industry ranks as a sales manager, general manager, and broker/ owner. Along the way, he developed residential subdivisions and completed significant adaptive re-use projects and commercial buildings.

He was CEO of Corporate Relocation Services (CRS) from 1985 to 2010, where he led a team of people to provide real estate consulting services to large corporations with national operations. These companies regularly relocated employees to serve business purposes in different locations. In this role as consultants, the CRS team worked with thousands of employees, real estate agents, appraisers, mortgage lenders, inspectors, and specialty contractors throughout the country.

In 1989, he founded a real estate company that was organized and developed to deploy a totally innovative business model for real estate services that significantly improved the customer experience. This model transformed the traditional real estate model to be similar to the way most other businesses in other industries deliver their products and services to the market.

Montgomery has been married for more than fifty years, and he and his wife, Mary Jo, have two grown children and a granddaughter, Magnolia Grace Montgomery. They live in Green Bay, Wisconsin, in the summer and Phoenix, Arizona, in the winter.

He enjoys nature, reading, writing, art, and walking and has a variety of interests from billiards and golf, to photography and clay sport shooting and Scrabble. He supports a number of charities devoted to helping children in need.

Made in the USA
Coppell, TX
14 September 2021

62327029R00089